OSPREY COMBAT AIRCRAFT • 77

# US NAVY
# A-1 SKYRAIDER UNITS
# OF THE VIETNAM WAR

SERIES EDITOR: TONY HOLMES

OSPREY COMBAT AIRCRAFT • 77

# US NAVY
# A-1 SKYRAIDER UNITS
# OF THE VIETNAM WAR

## RICHARD R BURGESS & ROSARIO M RAUSA

OSPREY
PUBLISHING

**Front cover**
On 7 February 1968, Lt Cdr Rosario 'Zip' Rausa and his wingman, Lt Larry 'Legs' Gardiner, launched in two VA-25 A-1H Skyraiders at 0700 hrs from USS *Coral Sea* (CVA-43). They were tasked with flying a close air support mission in aid of the US Special Forces camp at Lang Vei, five miles southwest of the Marine Corps base at Khe Sanh. Lang Vei was being overrun by North Vietnamese troops, whose assault was being supported by PT-76 tanks in their first use in South Vietnam. As the A-1 pilots headed inland, they were told over the radio that US soldiers were pinned down in a bunker.

Upon arriving over Lang Vei, which was ablaze with several fires, the VA-25 section encountered an overcast. However, a USAF Forward Air Controller (FAC) in an O-2A that was marshalling strike aircraft in the target area told them that the situation in Lang Vei was critical, and requested that the A-1 pilots strafe all positions in the camp. As the weather improved slightly, the A-1s broke air wing-required weather restrictions, followed the O-2A through a hole and, at 300-ft intervals, strafed the camp. Rausa (in 'Canasta 406', A-1H BuNo 137622) and Gardiner attacked with 250-lb Mk 81 and 500-lb Mk 82 bombs, releasing their ordnance at altitudes of between 300-500 ft. As the weather improved still further, the A-1 pilots dropped their bombs from a height of 1000 ft, and also made another strafing run.

After a short while, Rausa and Gardiner were relieved by two USAF A-1Es, carrying napalm and cluster bombs. Both A-1Hs had taken hits from small arms. Four more VA-25 Skyraiders also attacked Lang Vei with napalm later that same day, 'mopping the place up' and clearing a path of fire to the outpost gate that allowed seven American soldiers to escape (*Cover artwork by Mark Postlethwaite*)

First published in Great Britain in 2009 by Osprey Publishing
Midland House, West Way, Botley, Oxford, OX2 0PH
443 Park Avenue South, New York, NY, 10016, USA
E-mail; info@ospreypublishing.com

Print ISBN 13: 978 1 84603 410 7
PDF e-book ISBN: 978 1 84603 870 9

Edited by Tony Holmes
Page design by Tony Truscott
Cover Artwork by Mark Postlethwaite
Aircraft Profiles by Jim Laurier
Index by Michael Forder
Origination by United Graphics Pte
Printed in and bound in China through Bookbuilders
09 10 11 12 13    10 9 8 7 6 5 4 3 2 1

For a catalogue of all books published by Osprey please contact:
North America
Osprey Direct, C/O Random House Distribution Center, 400 Hahn Road, Westminster, MD 21157
E-mail: uscustomerservice@ospreypublishing.com

ALL OTHER REGIONS
Osprey Direct, The Book Service Ltd, Distribution Centre, Colchester Road, Frating Green, Colchester, Essex, CO7 7DW, UK
E-mail: customerservice@ospreypublishing.com
**www.ospreypublishing.com**

ACKNOWLEDGEMENTS
Special thanks to Wayne Mutza and Robert F Dorr for sharing their extensive photo collections. Also, thanks to A-1 Skyraider pilots Jerry Tabrum, George Carlton, Gordon Wileen, Cliff Johns, Gordon H Smith, Norm Lessard, Gary Gottschalk, J M Watson and Kendall Moranville, EA-1F electronic countermeasures officer Van Calcott, Roy Grossnick, Ed Marolda, Mike Walker, Curtis Utz, Steve Hill, Mark Evans, Gwendolyn Rich, Judy Walters, Morgan Wilbur, Sandy Russell, Wendy Leland and Joe Gordon of the Naval Historical Center, M Hill Goodspeed of the National Museum of Naval Aviation, Jan Jacobs and Doug Siegfried of The Talihook Association, Rick Morgan, Tom Hansen, Tom Chee, Angelo Romano, Peter Mersky, Rich Dann, Ed Barthelmes, Robert L Lawson, Hal Andrews, Stephen L Miller, Michael Grove, Dan Medeiros, Jack Long, Robert Olen, Norman Polmar and Rene Francillon.

# CONTENTS

# INTRODUCTION

In 1959, only five years had elapsed since France had given up its campaign to hold onto its colony of French Indochina. The region had duly been split into the kingdoms of Laos and Cambodia and the nation of Vietnam (the latter into North and South) by the Geneva Peace Conference. In 1959, the ruling Communist Party in North Vietnam, led by Ho Chi Minh, decided to begin a low-intensity infiltration to conquer South Vietnam. The decision marked the beginning of a 15-year campaign – ultimately successful – to reunite the country under communist party rule.

The North Vietnamese would eventually encounter resistance to their plans for expansion in the south from US forces stationed in the Far East during the 1950s and 1960s. These forces had stopped the North Korean invasion of South Korea in 1950, and then fought the Chinese to a stalemate along lines close to the original border between the two warring nations prior to a truce being declared in late July 1953.

The aircraft carrier task forces of the US Seventh Fleet had played a significant role in the conflict with communist forces in Korea, as well as in confrontations with the Chinese in the Formosa Strait during the 1950s. Flying from the decks of those carriers was an attack aircraft that remained largely unsung at the time, but which was subsequently credited by military historians as being the most effective combat aircraft of the Korean War.

The piston-engined Douglas AD (later A-1) Skyraider, which could carry heavier payloads than the more glamorous jet-powered contempo-

VA-122 A-1H BuNo 135251 poses for airshow photographers at NAS Lemoore, California, in May 1967. VA-122 'Spad School' provided type training for Skyraider pilots for the fleet from 1959 until late 1967, when it assumed the role of training A-7 Corsair II pilots and became 'Corsair College'. This Skyraider has only two 20 mm cannon installed – a common practice for a training unit (*Roger F Besecker via Robert F Dorr collection*)

raries that it shared the flightdeck with, soldiered on long after the Korean War had ended. The Skyraider – largely ignored in the popular media – outlasted most of the 'flash-in-the-pan' jets that came and went during the 1950s and early 1960s. At some point the nickname 'Spad' (a hark-back to the World War 1 French pursuit aeroplane) stuck to the Skyraider.

The seeds of the Skyraider's demise, however, were also sown in the war in which it shone so well. Korean War operations forced the US Navy to recognise the need for a truly all-weather night-attack aircraft – a recognition that eventually brought forth the legendary Grumman A2F (A-6) Intruder carrier-based attack aircraft. Reaching initial operational capability in 1963, the A-6A began rapidly replacing A-1H and A-1J Skyraiders in frontline US Navy attack squadrons.

The number of frontline Skyraider squadrons declined significantly during the late 1950s when the Air Task Groups (ad-hoc carrier air groups set up to meet the operational demand that exceeded the availability of statutory CVGs) were deactivated. By January 1960, the US Navy's air arm included just 14 frontline carrier-based attack squadrons equipped with AD-6/7 (later A-1H/J) Skyraiders:

| Atlantic Fleet | Pacific Fleet |
|---|---|
| VA-15 'Valions' | VA-25 'Fist of the Fleet' |
| VA-35 'Black Panthers' | VA-52' Knightriders' |
| VA-65 'Tigers' | VA-95 'Skyknights' (later 'Green Lizards') |
| VA-75 'Sunday Punchers' | VA-115 'Arabs' |
| VA-85 'Black Falcons' | VA-145 'Swordsmen' |
| VA-176 'Thunderbolts' | VA-152 'Friendlies' (later 'Wild Aces') |
| VA-196 'Main Battery' | VA-215 'Barn Owls' |

The number briefly grew to 16 units with the formation of two new squadrons during the course of 1960-61. VA-135 'Thunderbirds' was established at Naval Air Station (NAS) Jacksonville, Florida, on 21 August 1961 in response to the 1961 Berlin Crisis, but it was disestablished on 1 October 1962. VA-165 'Boomers', which had been established on 1 September 1960 at NAS Jacksonville, Florida, and moved to NAS Moffett Field, California, in September 1961, lasted considerably longer, seeing combat following its shift to NAS Alameda, California, in March 1964.

## REPLACEMENT TRAINING

Until September 1965, student naval aviators destined to fly the Skyraider were introduced to the aircraft while in the advanced phase of their undergraduate flight training. Aviation Training Unit 301 (later VT-30) at NAS Corpus Christi, Texas, was the sole such training squadron, and it was equipped with Skyraiders marked up in orange and white Training Command paint schemes.

The Atlantic Fleet had two replacement training sites for the AD. VA-42 'Green Pawns' at NAS Oceana, Virginia Beach, Virginia, trained pilots for Oceana-based Skyraider squadrons, but it began instructing Intruder crews from September 1963. Later that same month it got rid of its last A-1H. VA-42 continued to provide instrument training for Skyraider pilots until March 1964, however, when it transferred out its last multi-seat A-1E.

VA-44 'Hornets' at NAS Cecil Field, Florida, which had assumed the role of replacement training for the A4D (A-4) Skyhawk carrier-based light attack aircraft in 1958, also took on AD replacement training from January 1959 for units based in the Jacksonville area. In February 1963, however, the A-1 section was established as a separate squadron, namely VA-45 'Skyhawks'. The latter conducted training for future Skyraider crews until 1965, when the rapidly diminishing number of Atlantic Fleet A-1 squadrons resulted in the unit eventually switching to the TA-4F Skyhawk.

VA-122 'Spad School' was redesignated from VA(AW)-35 on 29 June 1959 at NAS North Island, California, when the squadron's mission was changed from all-weather attack to replacement training for Pacific Fleet Skyraider squadrons. The squadron moved to NAS Moffett Field in July 1961 and then to NAS Lemoore, California, in January 1963. VA-122 duly trained Skyraider pilots and maintenance crews, including some for the (South) Vietnamese Air Force (VNAF). It eventually received its first A-7A Corsair II attack aircraft in November 1966, and phased out A-1 training the following year.

VA-125 'Rough Raiders' was a replacement training unit for Pacific Fleet A-4 squadrons, although it also operated a few A-1E Skyraiders for instrument training until the arrival of the two-seat TA-4F Skyhawk in 1966.

Airborne Early Warning (VAW) squadrons that flew the EA-1E radar early warning version and EA-1F electronic countermeasures version conducted their own type training.

## DIMINISHING LINE-UP

As previously mentioned, once the A-6 transition began, the number of Atlantic Fleet A-1 attack squadrons rapidly declined. In the space of two years, four (VA-35, VA-65, VA-75 and VA-85) had converted to the A-6A. VA-35 made its final deployment with Skyraiders on board USS *Saratoga* (CVA-60) to the Mediterranean in November 1964, returning home in July 1965 and commencing its transition to the A-6A the next month.

VA-15, made its final deployment with Skyraiders on board USS *Franklin D Roosevelt* (CVA-42) to the Mediterranean in 1964 and then switched to the A-4B Skyhawk light-attack aircraft from August 1965. The transition of VA-15 to the A-4B instead of the A-6A was influenced by the pressing need for light attack units due to the rapid acceleration in combat operations in Vietnam and the greater availability of Skyhawks at that time.

In the Atlantic Fleet, that left VA-176, under the command of Cdr George D Edwards Jr, as the sole A-1 unit. Based at NAS Jacksonville, the 'Thunderbolts' deployed with Carrier Air Wing 10 (CVW-10) on board USS *Shangri-la* (CVA-38) to the Mediterranean on 10 February 1965, returning on 20 September 1965. Cdr Robert J Martin assumed command of the unit on 8 October 1965. VA-176 would subsequently join its Pacific Fleet sister squadrons at war in Vietnam.

# INTO VIETNAM

In early 1960, as US advisory presence increased in South Vietnam, Adm Harry D Felt, commander-in-chief of the US Pacific Fleet, said, 'By God, we're gonna put ADs in there'. That September, the first six of 25 AD-6s were sent to Bien Hoa airfield, near Saigon. A pilot/advisor, along with six enlisted men, was assigned to help teach the VNAF how to fly and maintain the attack bomber. The pilot was Lt Ken Moranville, the sole individual selected from a pool of 40 volunteers from ATU-301.

A demanding instructor, Moranville was widely recognised as being an aggressive pilot with a reputation for being a perfectionist. Having helped train the initial cadre of six VNAF pilots qualified to fly the AD-6 at NAS Corpus Christi, he took to the task in Saigon with relish.

'The Vietnamese were flying 'on-call' strike missions', he recalled. 'The Viet Cong (VC) were terrorising villages, quite often at night. Although we didn't fly after dark, the unit launched at dawn to check out VC positions. L-19 spotter aeroplanes flown by the VNAF were a big help. Generally, there was one division of four A-1s airborne at all times during the day, while another division remained on alert status near the runway.'

The Skyraider's typical ordnance load at Bien Hoa included two napalm bombs, 500-lb general-purpose 'iron' bombs and 2.75-in Folding-Fin Aerial Rockets (FFARs), normally carried in pods of 19 chambers each. These rockets could be fired singly or in salvo.

'I remember demonstrating the AD's firepower before a group of military leaders one day soon after arriving at Bien Hoa', said Moranville. 'I carried a full load of rockets and bombs. I took off and made a few runs at a simulated target on the field. On one of the dives I simultaneously fired eight pods full of rockets – 152 in all. They really threw up the dust. And when the ordnance was gone I flew a loop to a landing, taxied up to the line of VIPs almost like an ice-skater skidding to a stop, shut down the engine and jumped out of the cockpit all smiles. I couldn't help showing off a bit, and must admit I got a kick out of seeing the guests with their jaws agape in awe of the Skyraider's capabilities.

'In those early days the war was pretty much a Monday through Friday, daytime only, conflict. This was sort of an unwritten agreement between the opposing forces, perhaps because the participants had been at each others' throats for years, and there was no end in sight to the fighting, or resolution of the differences that stood between them.'

Although of poor quality, this rare photograph, taken at NAS Corpus Christi in mid-1960, show the first six pilots to be qualified to fly the AD-6, along with their US Navy instructor Lt Ken Moranville (*K E Moranville*)

One day in November 1960, six Skyraiders and six F8F Bearcats (also flown by the VNAF) launched in a hurry to prevent being overrun by an approaching, company-sized column of soldiers who intended to seize the airfield. They were elements of a coup d'etat attempt to oust South Vietnamese President Ngo Dinh Diem. As a dialogue continued between a general leading the column and a major representing the airfield units, the CO of the squadron dove at the column, flying his Bearcat low over the area between the head of the column and the gate to the base. He released a napalm bomb that scattered the column. He was followed by other Bearcats and the Skyraiders, swooping down and threatening the column primarily with the hearty roar of their engines and the ordnance on their pylons. Amazingly, this show of force worked.

As Moranville described it, 'It's hard to believe, but in the moments that followed, those troops were herded into a compound on the base by the Skyraiders and Bearcats circling overhead. Apparently, the sight of the heavily armed aeroplanes convinced the general to capitulate. I have to believe that that was the first, and probably only, time the Skyraider and the Bearcat were used like cowboys rounding up cattle into a corral'.

The coup failed, and President Diem remained in office, only to be assassinated three years later.

Later, flying a Bearcat, the CO of the unit Moranville was training crashed and was killed during a napalm attack on the VC. When the squadron located the wreckage, it appeared that one of the Bearcat's wings had been blown off in flight. Incredibly, a charred bazooka was found in the debris. It was theorised that a very brave communist soldier had stood in the path of the low-flying Bearcat and shot it down, before perishing himself in the ensuing crash. 'The crash had serious repercussions amongst the other flyers', Moranville recalled. 'The Vietnamese were very superstitious about such things, and they no longer wanted to fly Bearcats in combat. The Skyraider became their favourite aeroplane'.

VT-30 also trained 50+ VNAF Skyraider pilots at Corpus Christi in the early 1960s following the delivery of additional A-1s to the VNAF as the conflict escalated in its ferocity. Eventually, it was decided to conduct all training in South Vietnam, and this led to VA-125 detaching half of its personnel and 13 A-1H/Js to Bien Hoa. Known as Detachment Zulu, it began training VNAF pilots and maintenance crews on 24 April 1964, and remained in-country until 30 November. The detachment later flew dual-control A-1Es assigned to the VNAF.

Det Zulu initially trained VNAF pilots with the 33 A-1s that were present in South Vietnam, but attrition during its assignment meant that only 19 remained in-country by the time the detachment departed.

Meanwhile, back at NAS Alameda, VA-152 (led by Cdr H F Gernert) transferred from CVW-15 to CVW-16 on 1 October 1964 in preparation for its deployment on board USS *Oriskany* (CVA-34).

## PROJECT *WATERGLASS*

The first US Navy Skyraider squadron to deploy to South Vietnam was not an attack squadron but a detachment from Airborne Early Warning Squadron 13 (VAW-13). Its AD-5Q (EA-1F) electronic countermeasures aircraft found themselves employed not in jamming hostile radars but in an unfamiliar role as night interceptors.

In March 1962, reports of low-flying aircraft entering South Vietnamese airspace at night near the city of Pleiku, in the central highlands, prompted fears that the Viet Cong were receiving supplies via clandestine flights involving aircraft such as the AN-2 'Colt' biplane. The Joint Chiefs of Staff ordered the US Navy and USAF to identify which aircraft could best counter the low flyers. The latter selected the F-102 Delta Dagger jet interceptor. The US Navy chose an aircraft from the other end of the speed spectrum – the slow-moving AD-5Q.

This choice was more grounded in wisdom than might at first be assumed. Ten years earlier, the Marine Corps had successfully used radar-equipped Skyraiders in night intercepts over Korea. Although the US Navy had phased out its night-attack AD-5Ns in 1959, the AD-5Qs were converted from AD-5Ns. Fitted with ground-mapping APS-31 and air-intercept APS-19 radars, they were ideal for the night interceptor role.

In May 1962, VAW-13 had three AD-5Q detachments deployed in the Western Pacific on board USS *Hancock* (CVA-19), USS *Lexington* (CVA-16) and USS *Coral Sea* (CVA-43). Seventh Fleet commander Vice Adm William A Schoech objected to the detachment of these aircraft to South Vietnam, as they were the only electronic jamming platforms then available to the carrier air wings. However, Adm John H Sides, Commander-in-Chief, US Pacific Fleet, deferring to the urgency of the requirement, overruled Schoech's objection and ordered the deployment of AD-5Qs to South Vietnam under the project name *Waterglass*.

On 7 May 1962, Schoech duly ordered VAW-13 to establish Detachment 1 at NAS Cubi Point, in the Philippines. Six AD-5Qs from *Hancock* and *Coral Sea* were sent ashore to Cubi to begin training with USAF GCI (ground-controlled intercept) radar. Det One was ready for deployment in-country by June. Sides proposed that three aircraft be based at Pleiku, but the commander of US Military Assistance Command Vietnam decided to send the aircraft to Tan Son Nhut.

After an F-102 detachment completed its first deployment (Project *Candy Machine*), VAW-13 Det 1 sent three AD-5Qs – commanded by Lt Wallace A Shelton – to Tan Son Nhut on 10 August. The aircraft were fitted with four M3 20 mm cannon – two per wing – that were not normally installed in peacetime. The cannon were also fitted with flash suppressors. Soon, five crews were in place, beginning a rotation of three crews on alert, one performing administrative duties and one off duty.

US interceptors were authorised to down hostile aircraft over South Vietnam. Det 1 performed 399 practice intercepts, of which 366 were deemed successful. Although no hostile aircraft were encountered by the time Det 1 returned to Cubi Point on 21 September 1962 (when relieved by an F-102 detachment), it was considered a success. Adm H D Felt, Commander-in-Chief, US Pacific Command, stated;

'The EA-1F (AD-5Q) has proven to be highly suitable to the air

An EA-1F of VAW-13 Det 1 is seen between sorties at NAS Cubi Point on 4 February 1963. The four-seat electronic countermeasures version was known variously as the 'Queer Spad', 'Electric Spad', 'Fat Spad' or 'Left-Handed Spad', the latter because it had only one set of flight controls in the front cockpit. Det 1 supplied the cannon-armed EA-1Fs that flew night intercept patrols in northern South Vietnam during Operation *Water Glass* in 1962-63 (*US Navy via Wayne Mutza collection*)

defence mission in the Republic of Vietnam. It has demonstrated a high intercept probability (consistently above 90 per cent); it has flight performance characteristics compatible with pursuit and identification of slow targets; and it is equipped with four 20 mm cannon that can be fired accurately using (onboard) radar or visual sight. It can be effectively used on combat air patrol missions, and can be deployed to airfields with minimum support facilities and short runways.'

VAW-13 Det 1 returned to Tan Son Nhut on 3 January 1963 for a second *Waterglass* deployment that lasted until 17 February 1963. A third detachment was scheduled to relieve a *Candy Machine* deployment on 1 May, but it was cancelled by Sides after Vice Adm Thomas H Moorer, now Commander, US Seventh Fleet, objected to *Waterglass*. Like his predecessor Adm Schoech, Moorer stated that these detachments placed a strain on resources, and they deprived the fleet of electronic warfare training and readiness that were vitally needed in view of the increasing Soviet threat in the region. Also citing the fact that no hostile aircraft had been detected to date, he recommended termination of *Waterglass*.

Felt, however, continued to consider the requirement for interceptors to be valid, and eased Moorer's concerns by adding two more EA-1Fs to Det 1, bring the total number of aircraft in the detachment to seven. *Waterglass/Candy Machine* deployments resumed on a random basis in September 1963. F-102s deployed in October for two weeks, and VAW-13 Det 1 sent an EA-1F detachment to Tan Son Nhut in November for a week for what proved to be the last *Waterglass* operation.

## YANKEE TEAM AND PIERCE ARROW

On 2 August 1964, the attack by North Vietnamese Navy patrol boats on the destroyer USS *Maddox* (DD-731) in the Tonkin Gulf precipitated the first combat strikes of the Vietnam War for US Navy Skyraiders. It was the beginning of what was to become almost four years of intense action for A-1 units over Southeast Asia.

VA-52 'Knightriders', under the command of Cdr George H Edmundson, was on a routine deployment with CVW-5 on board USS *Ticonderoga* (CVA-14) when it was called on to commence flying missions in support of *Yankee Team* operations. The latter, which began on 19 May 1964, was a reconnaissance operation conducted by USAF RF-101 Voodoos and US Navy RF-8 Crusaders at low-level over North Vietnamese infiltration routes in Laos. This operation had already incurred losses, for on 6 June a VFP-63 RF-8A from USS *Kitty Hawk* (CVA-63) had been downed over Laos. Pilot Lt Charles F Klusmann was captured, but he escaped two months later. The next day, an escorting F-8D was downed, although pilot Cdr Doyle W Lynn was rescued.

From 1 July through to 1 August, the 'Knightriders' flew 157 *Yankee Team* sorties that included weather reconnaissance, rescue combat air patrol (RESCAP) and actual search and rescue (SAR) missions.

VA-145, deployed with CVW-14 on board USS *Constellation* (CVA-64), joined in *Yankee Team* operations in June. From that month until January 1965, the 'Swordsmen' – under the leadership of Cdr H A Hoy – also flew RESCAPs over South Vietnam and Laos.

The 2 August Tonkin Gulf incident mentioned earlier, in which three North Vietnamese *Swatow*-class patrol boats attacked the *Maddox*, added

Lt Cdr Lawrence Brumbaugh climbs into the cockpit of a VA-52 A-1H on board *Ticonderoga* on 13 August 1964, eight days after the commencement of Operation *Pierce Arrow* – the retaliatory strikes against North Vietnam following the Tonkin Gulf incidents. VA-52 lost no aircraft in the raids. The 'Knightriders' would return to the Tonkin Gulf the following year, again on board *Ticonderoga*, for intensive operations in Operation *Rolling Thunder* (*US Navy/PH3 R L White*)

Two A-1Hs from fly near their ship, USS *Constellation* (CVA-64), in the Tonkin Gulf on 12 August 1964 – exactly a week after the squadron's ill fated strikes against North Vietnamese targets on 5 August. The latter were made in retaliation for the 2 August attack and 4 August perceived attack on US Navy destroyers by North Vietnamese torpedo boats. VA-145 pilot Lt(jg) Richard Sather was shot down and killed during the strikes, thus becoming the first naval aviator to be lost in action in the Vietnam War. This combat deployment was *Constellation*'s only one with an A-1 attack squadron embarked. The aircraft leading this section (BuNo 139662) was subsequently issued to the VNAF after its retirement from US Navy service (*US Navy via Robert F Dorr collection*)

unexpected excitement to already tense *Yankee Team* operations. The three *Swatows* were damaged by 20 mm cannon fire from four of CVW-5's F-8Es. A second 'attack' on the night of 4 August – which turned out to have been imagined by the tense crews of the destroyers – met with a response launched from *Ticonderoga*, and included Cdr Edmundson and his wingman, Lt Jere A Barton, from VA-52. Using flares, they investigated the radar contacts reported throughout the incident by *Maddox* and USS *Turner Joy* (DD-951), but sighted no patrol boats.

The 4 August perceived incident, however, convinced President Lyndon B Johnson to authorise retaliatory strikes. Operation *Pierce Arrow* was ordered, and VA-52 – which had flown 44 sorties in support of 'De Soto' patrols between 2 and 4 August – launched into war on 5 August. The 'Knightriders'' four retaliatory sorties, led by executive officer (XO) Cdr Lee T McAdams, orbited the carrier for an hour before heading to the North Vietnamese coast. The attackers were credited with destroying 90 per cent of the petroleum storage facilities at the port of Vinh without loss or damage to themselves.

VA-145 was not so fortunate. CVA-64 launched its two strike waves from a longer range as it raced from a port call in Hong Kong. Cdr Melvin D Blixt, who took command of the 'Swordsmen' the day after the 2 August attack, led a division of A-1s in the *Pierce Arrow* strike against the patrol boat base at Hon Gay. A second strike wave, along with A-4Cs from VA-144, attacked five patrol boats near Lach Chao estuary and Hong Me Island. Two vessels were hit, but two VA-145 aircraft were struck by anti-aircraft artillery (AAA) and the one flown by Lt(jg) Richard C Sather crashed into the water two miles offshore. He had been attacking two *Swatows* near Lach Thuong at the time, and perished when his A-1 hit the sea. Sather had become the first US naval aviator to be killed as a result of enemy action during the Vietnam War.

The wreckage of the Skyraider (BuNo 139760) came to rest in water shallow enough for salvage, and his body was recovered by the North Vietnamese and returned to the United States after the war.

VA-52 continued *Yankee Team* operations through to 14 August, and CVA-14 remained off South Vietnam until 31 August. When the vessel returned to the area on 5 October, VA-52 flew an additional 104 sorties in support of *Yankee Team* up until the 29th of the month, followed by 47 in November, before the ship headed home on the 27th. VA-145 returned home on 1 February 1965, only days before the second round of combat operations against North Vietnam (*Flaming Dart*) commenced.

Also participating in *Yankee Team* was VA-196 'Main Battery', led by Cdr J R Driscoll. The unit was flying from the deck of USS *Bon Homme Richard* (CVA-31) as part of CVW-19 at the time, the 'Bonny Dick' having deployed in January 1964. The vessel had operated in the Indian Ocean for much of its cruise, and was not on hand for the *Pierce Arrow* strikes. However, upon returning to the South China Sea, VA-196 flew *Yankee Team* missions from 31 August through to 8 October 1964.

On the day of the *Pierce Arrow* strikes, USS *Ranger* (CVA-61) departed California, bound for the South China Sea. Deploying with CVW-9 were the 'Green Lizards' of VA-95. Led by Cdr Dwight E DeCamp, it commenced *Yankee Team* operations in November 1964, providing RESCAP for photo-reconnaissance missions and striking targets in Laos.

## *BARREL ROLL* AND *FLAMING DART*

*Yankee Team* operations came to a halt in November 1964 after two USAF jets (an F-100 and an RF-101) were downed over Laos. Retaliatory strikes recommended by the Commander-in-Chief, US Pacific Command (CINCPAC) were not approved. However, the Joint Chiefs of Staff proposed, and President Johnson approved, a new strike and armed recon-naissance programme over southern Laos. The campaign, codenamed Operation *Barrel Roll*, began on 14 December 1964, and F-8s flew the US Navy's first strikes on 17 December. The primary intention of *Barrel Roll* was to pressure the North Vietnamese into ceasing their activities in Laos, but the operation failed because the communists merely considered it a continuation of *Yankee Team*.

VA-215 'Barn Owls', under the command of Cdr Donald E Brubaker, deployed with CVW-21 on board USS *Hancock* (CVA-21) on 21 October 1964 and joined in the *Barrel Roll* strikes from 28 December.

The US leadership decided to intensify *Barrel Roll* in January 1965. The US Navy's resumption of operations in-theatre began inauspiciously on 15 January when A-1H pilots attracted to campfires struck Ban Tang Vai village in southern Laos after straying some 25 miles off course from their intended target. Four villagers were wounded in the strike that destroyed five houses and damaged seven granaries. US ambassador to Laos William Sullivan temporarily suspended night attacks, and CINCPAC tightened the strike rules to 'unmistakable military activity'.

**Deckcrewmen perform checks on the landing gear and external fuel tank of a VA-95 A-1 aboard *Ranger* in the Tonkin Gulf on 24 March 1965 as the 'Spad' is readied for launch. VA-95 participated in the first strikes of the *Flaming Dart* and *Rolling Thunder* campaigns against North Vietnam. The 1964-65 cruise aboard CVA-61 was the only Skyraider deployment made by the 'Green Lizards' to Vietnam (*US Navy via Robert F Dorr collection*)**

On 7 February 1965, VC sappers attacked the barracks of US advisers in Pleiku, killing eight Americans and wounding 104. President Johnson ordered retaliatory strikes against North Vietnam, and as part of Operation *Flaming Dart I*, VA-95 and VA-215 participated in these missions. A second VC attack on an American barracks at Qui Nhon took place on 10 February, precipitating *Flaming Dart II* the following day. In this operation, VA-95 struck the Chanh Hoa barracks near Dong Hoi. All out war between US forces in the region and the North Vietnamese now seemed inevitable.

# ROLLING THUNDER AND *STEEL TIGER*

On 19 February 1965, following escalating VC attacks and North Vietnamese intransigence, President Johnson approved Operation *Rolling Thunder* – the gradually escalating air campaign designed to force North Vietnam to abandon its invasion of the south. The US Navy was to play a major part in *Rolling Thunder*, with CVW-9 participating in the first carrier-based strike of the campaign on 15 March. VA-95 was involved in this mission (it would take part in three *Rolling Thunder* strikes prior to CV-61 heading home on 12 April), which targeted an munitions depot in Phu Qui. The unit also suffered the only combat fatality of the operation when Lt(jg) Charles F Clydesdale hit the water and was killed after his A-1H (BuNo 135375) was struck by AAA.

On 9 April the unit struck the Tam Da railway bridge, destroying it during the course of two missions flown that day. Twenty-four hours later, VA-95 also downed the Kim Kuong Highway bridge on Route 8.

VA-215, led by Cdr Robert C Hessom since 1 March, was also engaged in combat operations from *Hancock* during this period. The unit flew a number of Alpha strikes as part of CVW-21, and also conducted day/night armed reconnaissance sorties and supported rescue missions.

The 'Barn Owls' suffered significant losses during the deployment, with Lt(jg) C E Gudmunson's A-1H (BuNo 139790) being the first combat casualty for CVW-21 on cruise. One of 70 aircraft participating in the US Navy's second *Rolling Thunder* strike, the Skyraider was hit during the pilot's sixth pass on the radar site at Ha Tinh on 26 March. Gudmunson managed to coax his battered aircraft to within five miles of the US base at Da Nang, and duly survived a crash-landing.

Squadronmate Lt(jg) Gerald W McKinley was not so lucky five days later, however, when 60 US Navy aircraft returned to the coastal radar sites at Vinh Son and Cap Mui Ron. McKinley perished when his A-1H (BuNo 137584) was downed by AAA on his second low-level pass.

Lt Cdr James J Evans was shot down (in BuNo 139721) on 2 April during an armed reconnaissance mission of the Ho Chi Minh Trail north of the Laotian town of Ban Muong Sen. Listed as missing,

VA-215 A-1H BuNo 137628 taxis by F-8 Crusaders on the flightdeck of USS *Hancock* (CVA-19) on 29 March 1965 prior to launching on a combat mission over North Vietnam in support of Operation *Rolling Thunder*. The aircraft is heavily armed with eight 250-lb Mk 81 low-drag general-purpose bombs and four Aero 7D 19-shot 2.75-inch rocket launchers. On its first of three Skyraider deployments to Vietnam, VA-215 lost five aircraft in aerial action and had seven more written off as a result of combat damage. This particular aircraft survived the cruise, however (*US Navy via Wayne Mutza collection*)

Evans' skeletal remains were handed over to the US government by the North Vietnamese in November 1971 and identified two years later. Lt(jg) James P Shea died on the night of 19/20 April during an armed reconnaissance mission when his A-1H (BuNo 139818) hit the ground whilst attacking a truck convoy near Phu Qui, 30 miles north of the Demilitarised Zone (DMZ). Finally, on 27 April the A-1H (BuNo 137545) flown by Lt(jg) S B Wilkes was hit in the port wing several miles south of the Mu Gia Pass in Laos. Despite the damaged wing catching fire, the young pilot managed to fly the Skyraider across Laos and into Thailand. Heading for Nakhon Phanom AB, Wilkes was forced to bale out just two miles short of the airfield.

In addition to these five losses, seven A-1s from VA-215 returned to CVA-19 with varying degrees of combat damage during the deployment.

## *STEEL TIGER*

The limited impact of *Barrel Roll* caused a re-evaluation of the air campaign over Laos. With *Rolling Thunder* underway, President Johnson also approved a new intensive air campaign codenamed Operation *Steel Tiger*, which supplanted *Barrel Roll* in southern Laos – *Barrel Roll* continued in northern Laos, however. CINCPAC ordered that *Steel Tiger* was to commence on 3 April 1965. The US Navy's first *Steel Tiger* mission was launched 48 hours later, when five A-1Hs (with four F-8s for flak suppression and combat air patrol) attacked truck routes in Laos. This campaign would run for many years, with US Navy A-1s frequently assigned to strikes. It was occasionally marred by bombing errors too. For example, on 29 September 1965, two A-1s hit a target southeast of Thakhek, some 30 miles from the intended target. Further errors by USAF crews eventually resulted in a temporary suspension of *Steel Tiger*.

Most of VA-95's combat sorties during its time in-theatre were armed route reconnaissance flights in support of *Steel Tiger* and *Barrel Roll*, as well as RESCAP missions. Indeed, the unit suffered its second, and last, combat fatality on cruise during a *Steel Tiger* armed reconnaissance mission on 11 April 1965. Lt(jg) William E Swanson died when his A-1H (BuNo 135226) was stuck by AAA east of Ben Senphan. According to Swanson's wingman, his A-1 was hit and began to trail smoke as it lost height and crashed into the jungle canopy. The pilot may have been wounded, for he did not acknowledge calls made on the radio by his wingman, or attempt to bale out.

*Ranger* left the line the following day, taking VA-95 home from its only A-1 deployment of the war. The unit had flown 800+ combat sorties over Southeast Asia and dropped in excess of 659,000 lbs of ordnance at a cost of two A-1Hs and their pilots. The 'Green Lizards' left its A-1s at Cubi Point for eventual transfer to the VNAF and began transitioning to the A-4B Skyhawk at NAS Lemoore in July 1965.

An ordnanceman checks the payload of a VA-95 A-1 on board *Ranger* on 24 March 1965. This view of the starboard wing shows two M3 20 mm cannon, three Aero 7D 19-shot 2.75-inch rocket launchers and three Mk 24 illumination flares (*US Navy/PH1 Moesser*)

An unnamed VA-165 pilot examines the flak-damaged starboard wing flap of his A-1 on the deck of CVA-43 following a *Rolling Thunder* strike on 2 April 1965. The pilot is wearing his 'Mae West' life preserver and a pistol belt with a bandolier of bullets (*US Navy via Robert F Dorr collection*)

VA-165 'Boomers', having replaced VA-152 within CVW-15 during the latter squadron's 1964 training detachment in South Vietnam, deployed with the air wing on board *Coral Sea* on 7 December 1964 for what would prove to be the longest carrier cruise of the Vietnam War. The vessel would not return to Alameda until 1 November 1965.

The 'Boomers', under the command of Cdr R E Chamberlain (succeeded by Cdr A K Knoizen) saw considerable action in the *Rolling Thunder* strikes on North Vietnam in 1965, although the unit was spared the heavy losses of VA-215. In fact, it lost only two air-

craft and one pilot during 167 days on the line. The first of these was shot down on 13 August (the second day of its fifth on-line period) when Lt R J Hyland's A-1H (BuNo 139772) became the 15th aircraft from CVW-15 to be lost in combat on cruise.

Participating in an armed reconnaissance mission over the southerly provinces of North Vietnam, Hyland's formation attacked a group of trucks parked ten miles south of Vinh. His A-1H was severely damaged by ground fire as he bombed the vehicles, but again, the ruggedness of the Skyraider allowed Hyland to nurse his ailing aircraft some five miles out over the Tonkin Gulf before he took to his parachute. He was quickly rescued by a USAF HU-16B Albatross amphibian.

VA-165's only fatality came during yet another armed reconnaissance mission on 4 September 1965, when Lt(jg) Edward B Shaw's A-1H (BuNo 139693) was hit by AAA on his first attack run on a group of barges in the Song Gia Hoi River, 35 miles south of Vinh.

A VA-165 A-1 receives the launch signal from the catapult officer on board CVA-43. As denoted by its modex (NL 200), this aircraft was assigned to the commander of CVW-15. The aircraft is unusual in that it is equipped with a gun camera, located between the starboard landing gear and the starboard inboard wing pylon. Note also the Mk 54 350-lb depth bombs (with ringed tail fins) on the first outboard wing stations. These were frequently used against land targets (*US Navy/PH3 Koennenbecker*)

A-1H BuNo 134562, assigned to VA-165, is seen here parked on an apron at a base in CONUS on 16 October 1964. The aircraft was assigned to Lt(jg) Edward B Shaw, who was shot down and killed over North Vietnam in another A-1 on 5 September 1965 while flying a mission from CVA-43 (*US Navy via William L Swisher*)

## 'ELECTRIC SPADS'

VAW-13's Det 1, after a relatively quiet period of two years following the cessation of Project *Waterglass* in October 1963, continued to provide electronic countermeasures (ECM) support for carriers rotating for duty to the Seventh Fleet. As *Flaming Dart* and *Rolling Thunder* operations got underway in Vietnam, Det 1, with a complement of ten EA-1Fs, provided sub-detachments of two to four aircraft, eight to 16 officers, and 20 to 35 enlisted personnel to most carriers, including ships from the Atlantic Fleet sent to the Tonkin Gulf. Crews would serve with Det 1 for six-month periods before rotating home to Alameda.

As air operations over North Vietnam intensified, it was not

unusual for a Det 1 crew to launch on a mission as a carrier was ending a line period, and recover on a different carrier that had just arrived in-theatre.

EA-1Fs normally flew orbits off the coast of North Vietnam at altitudes of 8000-10,000 ft. Their role usually involved jamming the 'Whiff' and 'Fire Can' fire control radars of the enemy's AAA sites. The 'Queer Spad' could also jam the SA-2 'Guideline'

surface-to-air missile (SAM), but was limited in effectiveness. Two 20 mm cannon were carried, and EA-1F crews were known to risk their valuable aircraft to strafe watercraft.

While most ECM missions kept VAW-13's 'Electric Spads' out of harm's way, one fell victim to North Vietnamese AAA on 2 June 1965. The VAW-13 Det 1 aircraft from CVW-2, embarked in USS *Midway* (CVA-41), had flown toward the area to coordinate a SAR effort for a VA-23 A-4E pilot who had been downed while attacking a radar site near Thanh Hoa. The EA-1F (BuNo 132540) was hit as it approached the coast near Sam Son and exploded upon impacting the ground. The crew – Lt(jg)s M D McMican and Gerald M Romano and AT3s William H Amspacher and Thomas L Plants – were listed as missing and presumed dead (their remains were recovered after the war).

VAW-13 lost a second EA-1F (BuNo 135010) a year later on 20 June 1966 when the aircraft suffered bridle failure whilst being launched from *Hancock*. Pilot Lt John R McDonough died in the ditching, but the two other crewmen survived. Another VAW-13 EA-1F (BuNo 132543) was written off on 10 September 1966 when it suffered instrument failure and ditched in the Tonkin Gulf after exhausting its fuel searching for its carrier, USS *Franklin D Roosevelt* (CVA-42). The crew was rescued.

Engine failure left the crew of a VAW-13 Det 1 EA-1F (BuNo 133770) with no option but to ditch in the South China Sea during a ferry flight from NAS Cubi Point on 25 September 1967. They were rescued.

During the *Waterglass* operations and through to 1968, the 'Zappers' of VAW-13 conducted their own replacement crew training. The unit was typically equipped with about 20 EA-1Fs (including the Det 1 aircraft), an A-1G (October 1963 until January 1965) and, later, two A-1Es (one in June 1965 and the second four months later) for training. VAW-13 also possessed two EC-1A Traders for electronic threat simulation when training ships.

Crewmen service a VAW-13 Det 1 EA-1F on board a carrier in the Tonkin Gulf. An ALT-2/7 jamming pod can be seen beneath the folding section of the starboard wing, outboard of a multiple ejection rack armed with flares. The disc attached to the forward section of the ALT-2/7 pod is unusual, and its purpose is not known. This EA-1F is unusual for a US Navy Skyraider in that a black exhaust mask is painted behind the engine exhaust tubes – a practice common on early A-1Es and A-1Gs in USAF service (*US Navy via Robert F Dorr collection*)

A VAW-13 EA-1F recovers on board CVA-64 on 14 September 1967 after a combat mission in support of strikes over North Vietnam. The fuel dump tube can be seen extending from the underside of the Aero 1C external tank (*US Navy/PH2 A P Phillippi*)

# 'FIST OF THE FLEET'

In what was to become a memorable deployment, VA-25 'Fist of the Fleet', led by Cdr Ralph F Smith, embarked on board *Midway* with CVW-2 on 6 March 1965 and departed Alameda for Vietnam. The unit launched its first missions – RESCAP and SAR – on 10 April. Two days later, four VA-25 A-1s engaged enemy forces during a SAR mission over Laos, becoming the first *Midway* air crews to strike the enemy.

Almost daily, the 'Fist of the Fleet' launched RESCAP and road reconnaissance missions. On 15 April it participated in the saturation bombing of a VC stronghold in South Vietnam. The following day, Smith led a strike that destroyed the Bai Duc Tho highway bridge in North Vietnam.

On the night of Easter Sunday, 18 April, two VA-25 pilots on a road reconnaissance mission chanced upon a long convoy of trucks southwest of Vinh. Lt Cdr Harold E Gray Jr and Lt(jg) L O Woodbury made several runs on the convoy while reporting the contact to *Midway*. CVW-2 launched a large strike that worked over the convoy into the next morning. The scenario was repeated four nights later when Gray and Woodbury again spotted a 15-20 truck convoy.

VA-25 concentrated on road reconnaissance, road sensor 'seeding' and RESCAP, but on 23 April it joined other CVW-2 aircraft in attacking several bridges south of Vinh. On 28 April, a VAW-13 EA-1F detected PT boats in a river, and five VA-25 Skyraiders pounced on the vessels with napalm, claiming three of them sunk. The squadron finished April with a bomb and napalm strike against a supply depot south of Thanh Hoa.

On 1 May 1965 VA-25 began extensive operations against VC targets in South Vietnam, often under the direction of USAF FACs. On the 7th, the squadron covered the amphibious landing of US Marines at Chu Lai, where a new airfield was subsequently constructed. Thirteen days later, Smith led eight A-1s in a strike on the harbour at Vinh. The squadron was heavily engaged in road reconnaissance, hunting PT boats and 'seeding' sensors in the Mu Gia Pass during this period.

Smith was relieved by Cdr Harry E Ettinger as CO on 24 May, and the following day, eight VA-25 'Spads' demolished a military barracks. Shortly afterwards, a supply depot and a PT boat were also

Two A-1Js (left) and two A-1Hs approach their carrier, USS *Midway* (CVA-41), on 19 March 1965 with tailhooks lowered in preparation for recovery. The ship and its embarked air wing were en route to their first war deployment in the Tonkin Gulf when this photograph was taken. VA-25 launched its first combat mission on 10 April (*US Navy via Robert F Dorr collection*)

**A-1J BuNo 142048 of VA-25 drops a stick of 12 250-lb Mk 81 general-purpose bombs on a Viet Cong target northwest of Saigon in 1965 during the first Vietnam deployment of CVW-5 and CVA-41. Early in the conflict, it was common for carriers arriving in-theatre to conduct combat missions over South Vietnam to season the pilots with light opposition before they were launched over North Vietnam, and its dense air-defence network (*US Navy*)**

destroyed. Four more PT boats fell victim to VA-25 on 1 June, and on the 2nd the squadron dropped a span of a bridge near the Mu Gia Pass. On 4 and 5 June VA-25 'Spads' covered the successful rescue of a VA-22 A-4 pilot.

The 10 June strike on the Co Dinh thermoelectric powerplant, eight miles southwest of Than Hoa, resulted in VA-25's first combat loss. The XO, Cdr William J Stoddard Jr, led eight A-1s, accompanied by four A-4 flak suppressors, against this important target, with each aircraft making two runs. Lt(jg) James S 'Jim' Lynne scored a direct hit with a 2000-lb bomb that demolished the primary building. However, Lt(jg) Carl L Doughtie, who had been with the squadron only two weeks, died when his 'Spad' (BuNo 137521) hit a nearby hillside when it failed to pull out of its second dive-bombing attack. Doughtie's remains were recovered in 1997 by a Joint Task Force – Full Accounting (JTF-FA) investigation team.

A routine of road reconnaissance and RESCAP missions – as well as one eight-A-1 strike – followed in the days that led up to one of the Skyraider's greatest feats.

On 20 June, an F-105 pilot was downed by North Vietnamese AAA in the vicinity of Dien Bien Phu. *Midway* and CVW-2 were taking a rare day off, but the duty (RESCAP) from VA-25 was standing by, their Skyraiders at the ready. Shortly after receiving notification that there was a downed flyer in enemy territory, Lt Cdr Ed Greathouse and wingman Lt(jg) Jim Lynne, comprising the first section, and Lt Clint Johnson and Lt(jg) Charlie Hartman in the second, took to the skies, each carrying a typical RESCAP ordnance load – four 19-shot cylindrical pods of 2.75-in FFARs under the wings and full magazines of 20 mm cannon rounds.

Greathouse and his division went 'feet dry' flying at 10,000 ft, remaining 1000 ft beneath a lid of stratus cloud cover. The 10,000-ft height was considered reasonably safe in 1965, but a year later North Vietnam's expanding SAM threat would make that altitude too precarious. With visibility proving to be excellent, Greathouse directed the flight to adopt a 'combat spread'. He signalled the separate sections to move away from each other and fly parallel to his course, thus enhancing the formation's ability to manoeuvre and still maintain an effective lookout doctrine.

As they proceeded, the 'Spad' pilots were momentarily shaken by a transmission from a radar controller in a destroyer off the coast. '"Canasta" (VA-25's call-sign). There are bandits in the air'. At this point the A-1s were 50 miles northwest of Thanh Hoa, some 90 miles south of Hanoi. The controller radioed again. 'They are at your "six o'clock", at four miles. There are two of them, and the blips are merging together'.

Hartman recalled after the flight, 'It was after that call that I looked behind us and saw them. As the No 4 man, I was on Johnson's wing on the right flank of the formation. They were offset about one mile to the left, flying straight and level at about 10,500 ft. I don't mind telling you that my heart was really pumping. I was stunned. You don't see enemy fighters every day in your life. But there they were, a pair of silver MiG-17s heading roughly in the same direction that we were'.

Johnson, meanwhile, had lost his radios. Greathouse remembered, 'The MiGs were in right echelon. I believe they passed without seeing us. Jim Lynne and I spotted them at about our "seven" or "eight o'clock" and watched them continue on. Initially, I thought they might be

The four pilots of the VA-25 division that encountered two MiG-17 interceptors of the Vietnamese People's Air Force on 20 June 1965 over North Vietnam and downed one of them strike a celebratory pose in the 'Fist of the Fleet' ready room on board *Midway*. They are, from left to right, Lt(jg) Jimmy S Lynne, Lt Cdr Edwin A Greathouse, Lt Clinton B Johnson and Lt(jg) Charlie W Hartman (*US Navy/PH2 Hunze*)

headed toward another flight of "Spads" from VA-196, which was operating in the area ahead of us, but when the MiGs were about one-and-a-half to two miles ahead, they executed a rapid reversal toward my section.

'My guess is they didn't spot us at first because we were just below the overcast. Their radar operator on the ground probably realised that the MiGs had overshot. Their reversal was very likely a response to a call from their controller. I transmitted "Heads Up" to the flight as they turned.'

Hartman continues, 'The familiar story of the No 4 man being the first to be downed on an initial attack raced through my mind'. He was referring to tales of unseen fighters surprising a formation and knocking down its 'tail-end charlie' first. But in this case, after the MiGs turned, all the aircraft were confronting each other directly. The fight was about to commence. The two elements were approaching each other at a closing speed of 600 knots. The pilots' adrenalin was really pumping now. Greathouse, seeing the MiGs turn toward the Skyraiders, radioed an expletive. Then, instinctively, the A-1s executed split-S manoeuvres, diving for the trees.

The MiGs and the Skyraiders were now in a valley between two ridgelines that were nearly 2000 ft high. The landscape was hilly and interrupted by limestone peaks, called karsts, which poked up noticeably from the ground. A river ran through the valley, and the A-1 pilots began following it, staying below 500 ft and occasionally dipping to 50 ft above the treetops. They were in 'their environment', down low and slow, compared to the high-speed, high-altitude world of fast moving jets. Importantly, jets consumed much larger amounts of fuel at low altitudes, and this factor could serve to distract the MiG pilots somewhat.

When one of the MiGs seemed to be tracking directly toward Hartman's aircraft, Greathouse ordered the 'Spads' to release their 300-gallon drop tanks. For Hartman, this order was a real blessing, for as he punched off the tanks his Skyraider leapt seemingly straight up in the air from the sudden loss of weight just as bullets from the approaching MiG, identified by tracer rounds, ripped through the sky exactly where he had been an instant before. Johnson, seeing the tanks drop and the tracer rounds, thought for a moment that Hartman had been hit.

Inexplicably, the MiG that had just fired at Hartman sped by the two Skyraiders and executed a sharp turn toward the north as if he were departing the area. The 'Spad' drivers figured he might be running out of fuel. At this point, Hartman and Johnson were on the northern side of the formation, with Greathouse and Lynne near a karst to the south, jinking aggressively as the other MiG pursued them. The Skyraiders were 'bucketing' along at 225 knots, which was considered to be a very high cruise speed for the propeller-driven attack aeroplane, especially at low altitude.

The next few seconds were as critical as they were confusing. Hartman said it 'was like being in a mixmaster. There was a swirling fight involving four or five full-circle turns, with us trying to either stay out of the MiG's sights or get a shot at him. The MiG pulled up after the fifth circle. He then rolled sharply to the left in order to get into position for a head-on pass at Greathouse and Lynne. As he sped toward them, Johnson and I had a head-on shot at the MiG. We both fired our cannons'. A post-flight check indicated that Hartman fired about 90 rounds and Johnson 50.

Hartman added, 'I saw the MiG's canopy shatter as the shells struck both it and the fuselage, but the jet kept coming toward us, trailing a thin plume of flame and smoke. Its pilot was probably incapacitated, because the MiG flew between Johnson and I pretty much straight and level'.

Then, surprisingly, the jet fell off on its wing and slammed into the ridge. A red-and-black fireball erupted where the MiG had been. The fighter's partner was last seen disappearing into the distance. 'The whole affair lasted about three minutes', Hartman recalled. 'We joined up, excited as hell, and headed back to the ship. It was dark when we landed'.

It is Hartman's belief that when the MiG made his tight turn to gain a shot at Greathouse and Lynne, he either lost sight of or forgot about Johnson and himself. It was a rarity for a propeller driven aircraft to 'bag' a jet. The team concept paid huge dividends for this quartet of 'Spad' drivers.

Hartman and Johnson were awarded Silver Stars for their achievement, while Greathouse and Lynne received Distinguished Flying Crosses (DFCs). Greathouse continued his US Navy career, retiring as a captain. Hartman retired as a commander. Johnson subsequently became an airline pilot while Lynne lost his life in an aeroplane crash in Indonesia in the late 1970s while performing his duties as a flying missionary.

## RESCAPs AND SARs

As VA-25 continued its heavy schedule of operations, the unit lost another aircraft on 24 June. Returning from a combat mission, the A-1H (BuNo 137523) of Lt Cdr R L Bacon suffered an engine failure and the pilot was forced to ditch – he was rescued by a UH-2 flown by CVW-2's HU-1 Det A. Despite having lost two Skyraiders in two weeks, VA-25 maintained its punishing mission schedule. The unit finished its second line period on 27 June by bombing a mountainside that slid across a key road, blocking it with tons of debris. Upon returning to *Yankee Station* (the central location for carrier operations

VA-25's A-1H BuNo 139768 rests on the NAS Lemoore apron post-cruise. This aircraft was flown by Lt Clint Johnson on his MiG-killing mission of 20 June 1965. A MiG-17 silhouette and numerous mission markings can just be seen below the cockpit. (*US Navy via National Museum of Naval Aviation/Wayne Mutza collection*)

against North Vietnam) on 23 July, VA-25 destroyed four bridges. But RESCAP missions dominated the war for the 'Fist'. On 24 July, Lt(jg) Nick Daramus, who was new to the unit, was assigned as a wingman on a two-aeroplane RESCAP flight that was to be led by Lt Abe Abrahamson. Not long after they were airborne, a USAF rescue coordination aircraft, call-sign 'Crown Alpha', summoned the Skyraiders to provide help for an F-105 pilot who had ejected from his jet after being hit by AAA over Laos.

Despite the area being blanketed by thunderstorms, with clouds rising to 12,000 ft, Abrahamson adroitly led the flight down beneath the clouds that had created a meteorological 'lid' 800 ft above the landscape. The A-1s were now over a thickly forested expanse surrounded by hills.

'We located the survivor, although it took quite a while, even though he helped by transmitting to us on his survival radio', Daramus said. 'There's nothing quite so small and undetectable as a human being in the jungle. Abe and I had difficulty keeping each other in sight because of extremely poor visibility, and the need to keep a wary eye on the terrain. It wouldn't do to smash into one of those hills'.

The undergrowth over which the Skyraiders were flying was thick, but not very high. It featured tall grass and banana plants, with their sizeable leaves. The flyers located the pilot, who was hiding beneath one of the banana plants. That achieved, the A-1s moved out to the west to join the inbound helicopter, and then returned to the scene for the pick-up. All things considered, collecting the downed pilot was routine. There was ground fire, but it was intermittent, and quickly silenced by the Skyraider pilots using 2.75-in FFARs in conjunction with the 20 mm cannons.

'Abe and I were about to escort the chopper out of the danger zone', Daramus said, 'when "Crown Alpha" notified us that an Intruder had just been bagged (through the premature detonation of its Mk 82 bombs). Our helo pilot radioed his thanks and said, "We can find our way home okay. Don't worry about us". So we departed for the A-6 crew – a pilot and bombardier-navigator (BN), down in an area which my charts verified was noted for heavy concentrations of AAA and small arms fire. It was a place to be avoided whenever possible. Today it wouldn't be possible'.

Picking their way through clouds and the hilly landscape, the 'Spad' pilots encountered AAA but remained unscathed. The A-6 crew had landed in a clearing characterised by rice paddies in neat square-shaped patterns. The paddies seemed to be about two miles in width. The pilot was thought to be hiding amidst a cluster of small trees at the centre of the clearing, while the BN was in amongst large trees along the edge of it.

The A-1 pilots established radio communications with the survivors and figured out that the pilot and BN were nearly half-a-mile from each other. The pilot seemed to be in good physical condition, but the BN had a leg injury that inhibited his ability to move. Enemy ground troops were then sighted heading in the direction of the downed flyers.

'We were trying to pinpoint the survivors' locations by radio', Daramus continued. 'Had they used signal flares, they would have been like bright arrows pointing at their precise positions. The survivors called out movements of the troops. Abe, meanwhile, was trying to transmit their location to "Crown Alpha" so that a helo could be summoned. We didn't know it right away, but two Marine Corps "whirlybirds", based somewhere in South Vietnam, were on the way.

'At the same time, Abe and I made coordinated rocket and strafing runs, covering each other from ground fire, and trying to hold the oncoming forces at bay. Finally, Abe determined that there was simply too much chatter on the airwaves. "You'll have to stay off the radio for awhile", he cautioned the survivors, "or we won't be able to get you out".

'For about an hour we swooped and circled, effecting a stand-off with the enemy. We'd see people heading for the clearing from a nearby village. As they approached, Abe and I would roll in and strafe them. Rolling in was a job in itself because of the low overcast. It was very difficult to get a steep enough dive angle for accuracy. We'd have to pop up into the clouds in turns then poke down through, which didn't leave much time to track, aim and fire a burst or two before pulling up.

'The A-6 flyers were instrumental in securing their own rescue once we got the radio talk reduced. They would report "On Top" when Abe and I flew directly over them, thus enhancing our ability to know exactly where they were. But because they remained hidden in the foliage, we didn't see them until they finally fired tracers from their revolvers a little later.'

The 'Spad' flight had been on the scene for two hours when 'Crown Alpha' directed a helicopter into the clearing, the survivors' location having been pinpointed. Meanwhile, Daramus and Abrahamson were running low on ammunition, forcing them to make non-firing runs over the terrain to discourage enemy troops from moving toward the downed flyers. A second helicopter was subsequently ordered in, and Abrahamson escorted one and Daramas the other. At the last moment the Skyraider pilots directed the survivors reveal themselves so that the helicopters could swoop down and collect them.

'I must admit that the action now resembled that of a cage of excited monkeys', Daramus related. 'We had the two survivors, two helicopters and two "Spad" pilots all talking on the same frequency trying to achieve two separate pick-ups within the same area at the same time. We had kept the helicopters over the heavily forested hills, reducing their exposure to a minimum, until they made a final dash in. The survivors left their sanctuaries at the right time, even though they were reluctant to enter the clearing, knowing the bad guys were nearby. The pilot got to his helicopter in short order and clambered aboard. The BN took longer because of his injury, but he made it too.

'We then hustled out of there as fast as we could, but found it impossible to stay with the choppers because of the terrain and the poor weather. The helo pilots assured us that they could find their way home and motored off, unescorted, with two happy warriors on board. Abe and I joined up and headed home. We logged 7.8 hours in the saddle that day. What a great aeroplane to do it in. With the A-1, it was a piece of cake!'

On 27 July, Greathouse and Lynne were on rescue patrol when F-105Ds attacked two North Vietnamese SAM sites near Hanoi. No fewer than six Thunderchiefs and their pilots were shot down near the site, or on the way back to their base in Thailand. Greathouse recalled;

'Jim and I arrived for RESCAP duty around 1300 hrs, just as the last fighter was leaving the scene. There was only one "evader" on the ground, some 30 miles west of Hanoi. Visibility was so good that I could easily see the city and its airport from my location. There were several AAA batteries in the immediate vicinity, but the pilot was on a good-sized ridge.

'We communicated with him, pinpointed his location and told him to stay put while we left the area, as we did not want to give away his location to the enemy. We retired 60 miles to the south, close to the Laotian border, to await a helicopter. Every hour or so we would return and talk with the downed pilot for a few minutes. Finally, at about 1600 hrs, we were advised that a helicopter was on the way, but that it would be slow in coming because it had to refuel several times en route. It would arrive at dusk.

'The Jolly Green Giant arrived at the North Vietnamese border unescorted and ready to go to work, despite the fact that the pilot had no maps or knowledge of the area! Using our direction-finding gear, we "talked him" to our position near the Black River, spotted him and escorted the helicopter to the ridge, arriving as darkness was setting in.'

Several enemy trucks and ground troops arrived in the area at the same time as a flight of F-105s made their presence known. The North Vietnamese converged in the flat lands surrounding the high area, which was the survivor's temporary sanctuary. The CH-3C Jolly Green Giant paid out 200 ft of its rescue cable down through the jungle canopy, the crew doing a magnificent job concentrating on the task at hand despite the oncoming enemy troops, who were proceeding toward the survivor's location. The downed pilot managed to get into the sling and the Jolly Green Giant crew began reeling in the cable.

To the frustration of all on the allied side, the cable became fouled and would not retract more than 50 ft. The rescued pilot was left dangling 150 ft below the helicopter. With enemy troops moving closer, the pilot fortuitously sighted what looked like an abandoned military camp nearby. It had barracks-type structures and a parade ground. The F-105 pilot hung on as the helicopter pilot tried to land on the parade ground. To the continued frustration of all, however, a flagpole was so positioned as to prevent a safe touch down. The pilot in the sling got off as the CH-3C moved toward a rice paddy 300 ft away. He ran toward the moving helicopter.

'Because of the mud and water in the paddy, the helicopter couldn't sit down', Greathouse recalled. 'Its pilot moved away another 50 yards or so, looking for a better spot'. The survivor scampered after the Jolly Green Giant in a kind of race that would have challenged the most conditioned of Olympic runners. As Greathouse noted, 'That pilot was really high-stepping and splashing through there. The trucks were a mere quarter-of-a-mile away, rumbling toward the paddy. Jim and I and the F-105s kept them at bay with strafing runs'.

The suppression attacks worked, and a joyful Capt Frank J Tullo of the 12th TFS/18th TFW scrambled aboard the CH-3C, which promptly lifted off and flew away to safety. Although it was growing dark as Greathouse and Lynne escorted the helicopter to the Laotian border, the Jolly Green Giant pilot radioed that he could make it home on his own. Thus relieved, the 'Spad' drivers swung east toward *Midway*. Because they had been airborne for such a long period, CVA-41 directed the duo to proceed to Da Nang, land there and launch for the carrier the next day.

On 28 July, while heading up a strike near the Laotian border, Cdr Ettinger led a successful rescue for a VA-23 A-4 who had been shot down whilst providing flak suppression for the A-1s. That same day, two VA-25 pilots returning from a RESCAP station located the crew of a VF-21 F-4B after they had ejected 25 miles from *Midway*. The A-1s remained in

Two VA-25 Skyraiders (an A-1H at left and an A-1J), loaded with high-drag bombs, head for a target in North Vietnam in a hazy overcast on 21 August 1965. The A-1H seen in this photo is the aircraft flown by Lt Clint Johnson during his MiG-killing mission (*US Navy/Lt Cdr Keith Boyer via Robert F Dorr collection*)

This VA-25 A-1J, flown by squadron XO Cdr 'Bill' Stoddard, came to grief during a gear-up landing at Da Nang AB in 1965. Da Nang was the primary divert field for carrier operations over North Vietnam. Note the fire-suppressing foam on and around the aircraft. A-1Js, which served along with A-1Hs in US Navy squadrons, were easily distinguishable from H-models by their BuNos. All 72 A-1Js were assigned numbers beginning with 14, while A-1Hs were assigned numbers beginning with 13 (*USAF via Robert F Dorr collection*)

contact until the crew was rescued by an UH-2 from HU-1.

VA-25 continued a daily surveillance of North Vietnamese roads in August, destroying trucks and striking caves used for supply storage. On the 6th, an eight-aeroplane strike was flown against targets 100 miles west of Hanoi, and this was followed the very next day by another mission that was intended to hit Dien Bien Phu. Bad weather diverted the strike to the Dong Hoi Citadel, however, and the latter was severely damaged by the Skyraiders. The unit paid a high price for this success, for Lt Cdr Harold E Gray was killed when his A-1 (BuNo 135329) was hit by 37 mm AAA fire on his second run and the aircraft crashed into the target area. VA-25 hit Dien Bien Phu and Dong Hoi again during the next few days.

On 13 August CVA-41 headed south to *Dixie Station* for operations over South Vietnam. VA-25 welcomed the respite from the flak-infested North, flying close air support missions from the central coast to the Gulf of Siam. On 23 August *Midway* replaced *Coral Sea* for two days off North Vietnam, during which time CVW-2 hunted SAM sites. VA-25 flew many unsuccessful SAR sorties for the crews of a VF-21 F-4B and a VA-22 A-4C downed on 24 August – all three naval aviators became PoWs.

Following almost three weeks of non-operational flying, CVW-2 returned to *Yankee Station* on 15 September. The following day, Cdr Stoddard was wounded by AAA during a RESCAP mission, but he managed to force-land at Da Nang (in A-1J BuNo 142021). On 20 August, Ettinger and Woodbury located the downed pilot of a VA-72 A-4E and guided a UH-2 from HC-1 Det A (embarked aboard the cruiser USS *Galveston* (CLG-3)) to the rescue in the face of heavy AAA. This was the first overland rescue conducted by a US Navy helicopter in North Vietnam, and the first anywhere in Southeast Asia by a ship-based helicopter.

On 24 September Lts D R Laack and Jim Lynne silenced gun positions near Tiger Island, on the North Vietnamese coast, allowing an HU-16B to pick up an F-4C crew that had ejected over the channel after having been hit by AAA.

*Midway* headed down to *Dixie Station* once again on 1 October, and VA-25 flew a litany of missions against VC targets with bombs and napalm, destroying numerous structures, as well as hitting jungle areas under the direction of FACs. Returning to *Dixie Station* on 19 October for the last line period of

the deployment, VA-25 flew close air support missions for the Special Forces camp at Plei Me, which had been fighting for its survival against a fierce VC siege. On the 20th, four VA-25 'Spads' bombed and strafed a VC suicide charge at the camp's perimeter, moving the defenders to state 'that without the accurate air support in those first few critical hours, Plei Me would have undoubtedly been captured by the Viet Cong'.

Another mission on 23 October yielded a significant blow to the VC. Cdr Ettinger led a three-aeroplane strike against a section of road 30 miles south of Plei Me to clear the area for friendly troops, who subsequently found the bodies of 102 VC killed by the 'Spads'' bombs. Ettinger was also in the vanguard of a strike that destroyed 22 VC buildings near Saigon. Other missions in South Vietnam in October resulted in the destruction of 56 enemy buildings by 56 bombs.

On 4 November, Cdr Stoddard delivered the 6,000,000th pound of ordnance dropped by VA-25 during the deployment – a porcelain privy, complete with box fins and nose fuse. *Midway* turned for home that day, soon to begin a five-year modernisation period and eventual return to Vietnam long after the 'Spads' were gone.

*Midway* turns into the wind in the Tonkin Gulf for a launch of a strike over North Vietnam on 27 October 1965. Eight VA-25 A-1s are positioned on the aft flightdeck, most with wings unfolded. *Midway* deployed to the war in 1965, which was its only Vietnam Cruise before going through a major overhaul and expansion of its flightdeck (*US Navy/Lt(jg) R W Lewis*)

Cdr 'Bill' Stoddard, executive officer of VA-25, in NE 572 *PAPER TIGER II*, readies to launch in October 1965 from CVA-41 with a heavy ordnance load that includes a toilet appropriately marked with the squadron's 'Fist of the Fleet' insignia. The cracked toilet was about to be discarded by the carrier's crew when VA-25 decided to rig it to a bomb rack. According to Lt Clint Johnson, the squadron's flightdeck crewmen who conducted the final checks before launch stood between the toilet and the vessel's island superstructure to block the view from the carrier's air boss and skipper. The toilet was expended on a target in South Vietnam to mark the sixth millionth pound of ordnance dropped by VA-25 on its first Vietnam deployment. The drop was filmed by a 16 mm gun camera installed on an A-1 flown by Lt Cdr Robin Bacon. Later fleeting up to CO, Stoddard was killed during VA-25's second Vietnam deployment by an SA-2 SAM on 14 September 1966 (*National Museum of Naval Aviation via Wayne Mutza collection*)

27

# 152nd AT WAR

VA-152, self-styled as the '152nd Light Bombardment Squadron and Twilight Pursuit Squadron', departed Alameda on board USS *Oriskany* (CVA-34) under the command of Cdr Albert E Knutson on 5 April 1965. Part of CVW-16, it arrived on *Dixie Station* on 8 May for seven weeks of operations mostly over South Vietnam striking VC troop concentrations. On 18 June, operations shifted to North Vietnam, Laos and Thailand, and for two weeks a four-aeroplane detachment flew from Udorn AB, Thailand, assisting in the rescue of two USAF pilots. Operations then switched to South Vietnam from 3 to 18 July.

On 30 June and 21 July, VA-152 lost A-1Hs (BuNos 139708 and 139636, respectively) due to engine failures – both pilots were rescued.

Capt (then Lt) Gordon C Wileen described the changing war for the 'Spad' squadrons at this time;

'We stopped flying Alpha Strikes early on because we were much too vulnerable to SA-2s, and evasive tactics hadn't been developed yet. We flew armed "recce" (reconnaissance) missions both day and night, and pre-positioned RESCAP for Navy Alpha strikes. These RESCAP missions involved flying a medium altitude, fuel-conserving racetrack pattern just off the North Vietnamese coast, waiting to be called in to cover US Navy SH-3 "Big Mother" or USAF HH-3 Jolly Green helicopters, or the HU-16 Albatross aircraft, on aircrew extraction missions.

'It didn't matter where in North Vietnam the downed aircrew was located, we went in to get them out. And we got the hell shot out of us from ground fire and AAA. I returned from one mission, when I stayed down too low for too long, with 276 holes in the airframe of my "Spad".'

Wileen and his wingman Lt Jack Smith were assisting the same SAR effort when VA-25 scored its 20 June MiG kill;

'Jack and I saw it all as we were evading just above the treetops. Since all six of us (including Greathouse's division) had punched off our tanks, we didn't have enough fuel left to make it back to the ship, so we joined up with a USAF C-118 transport in near darkness and flew his wing into Udorn Air Base, where we landed 3.7 hours after leaving the ship.

'We were ecstatic over the MiG kill, and the USAF guys at Udorn celebrated with us. They took us into the nearby town to a clean little hotel and we drank ourselves to sleep with Singha beer. Next morning, the Seventh Air Force commandeered all six of us and teamed us up with Air America crews hunting for downed airmen. We flew two 4.5- to 6.0-hour missions each day until we were released back to US Navy control on

A VA-152 A-1H is tensioned on a catapult just before launching from *Oriskany* in 1965 during the carrier's first Vietnam deployment. Although the Skyraider was capable of deck-run take-offs without the assistance of a catapult, the heavy ordnance loads carried by the 'Spad' made use of the catapult most advantageous. A-1 pilots usually kept their cockpit canopies open when launching for easier egress in the event that the aircraft lost power and went into the water. The US Navy lost 21 Skyraiders of all types to mishaps during its Southeast Asia deployments between 1964 and 1968 (*US Navy*)

23 June. While at Udorn, an A-3 from *Oriskany* brought Jack Smith and me $20.00 and a toiletries kit. We had to pay for some fine meals in the Air America compound, and it was worth every cent.

'On another occasion in 1965, a division of "Spads" from *Oriskany* loaded with two 2000 pounders on the inboard racks and smaller bombs on the wing racks launched on a mission to bomb a large barracks and truck staging area in North Vietnam's Route Package I. The plan was to climb to 10,000 ft before going feet dry (over land) to stay just above the 37 mm AAA burst altitude. With that weapon load it took an eternity to reach 10,000 ft. Just before levelling off, the No 2 pilot yelled, "I'm hit, I'm hit!" over the UHF radio. We all looked around but didn't see any sign of AAA, so the flight leader eased his "Spad" back to look over the wingman's aeroplane. "No visible damage", he informed his wingman.

'It turned out that before the launch, the wingman had over inflated his "doughnut". A-1 pilots often sat on inner tubes (like those used by women during pregnancy) to ease the pain in their buttocks, especially on long flights. The "doughnut" expanded during the climb until it exceeded maximum pressure and exploded. We didn't know this at the time, so our lookout doctrine was intensified for the rest of the flight. The wingman did take a AAA hit in the canopy on another mission. Shards of glass struck his neck and upper torso, earning him a Purple Heart.'

VA-152 suffered its first pilot loss of the deployment on 10 August when Lt(jg) Lawrence S Mailhes crashed in his A-1J (BuNo 142012) due to unknown causes during a RESCAP mission near Tiger Island.

The unit participated in the rescue of other pilots on 11 and 24 August, but on the 26th it lost Lt(jg) Edward A Davis' A-1H (BuNo 139720) to AAA while attacking a truck park during a night road reconnaissance mission near Xuan Noa, 15 miles north of the DMZ. Davis baled out but was captured. He was one of only three US Navy A-1 pilots to become PoWs during the war, and was released after the ceasefire in January 1973.

Three days later, on 29 August, Lt Edd D Taylor was killed when his A-1H was hit by AAA during an unsuccessful SAR mission for a USAF F-105F pilot near Son La, 105 miles west of Hanoi. The Skyraider crashed in almost exactly the same some spot as the Thunderchief, which had fallen victim to small arms fire the previous day. It appears that the NVA had set a trap for the SAR team, as F-105 pilot Capt Wesley D Schierman was captured shortly after the A-1 was shot down.

On 30 September, *Oriskany* began a line period when RESCAP and armed reconnaissance missions predominated for VA-152. CVW-16 launched a series of Alpha strikes against heavily defended targets from 5 October. On the 17th, unit XO Cdr Gordon H Smith, Lt Cdr Paul G Merchant, Lt D L Clarke and Lt(jg) James A Beene flew cover for the unsuccessful rescue attempt of a VF-84 F-4B crew that had been shot down near Na Ling, on the Vietnam-China border. They were one of three Phantom II crews from CVW-7 downed during an Alpha strike on the Thai Nguyen road bridge, some 30 miles north of Hanoi.

Heavy fire directed at the rescue aircraft included the first SA-2s to be shot at A-1s during the war – a development that would eventually drive the 'Spad' from regular operations over North Vietnam.

On 1 November, Lt Wileen and Lt(jg) E R Boose sank a junk that was trying to pick up a USAF RF-101C pilot offshore from Haiphong. Their

VA-152 A-1H BuNo 139810 taxis toward a catapult past F-8E Crusaders of VF-162 and VMF(AW)-212 on the deck of *Oriskany*. The 'Spad' is armed with two 1000-lb box-fin bombs and four 500-lb low-drag bombs. The employment of large bombs by A-1 units was common in 1965-66 until the growing SAM threat discouraged the use of Skyraiders on strike missions against targets in North Vietnam (*Gary Gottschalk via Wayne Mutza collection*)

efforts allowed an HU-16B to safely extract the pilot.

'By the autumn of 1965, each pilot in the squadron was a seasoned veteran with more than 100 combat missions', Cdr Smith recalled. 'We had been in the Tonkin Gulf for more than six months, and almost all of our flying had been into North Vietnam. We had spent a week or two in the south at the beginning of the tour, and when we moved to the north we soon learned that there was a world of difference between the two in terms of survival. We also learned that the north was no place for the "Spad", especially in Route Packages IV, V and VI.

'Our mission at those times was pretty much the same as that of the A-4s, except for the added responsibility of SAR. By then we had gained a reputation for being a "bunch of tigers" in the SAR game, having led the effort in 12 successful rescues. Some of our reputation was well deserved, but much of it was derived from a combination of luck and hype.

'Two years earlier, while on a so called "non-combat" cruise aboard *Hancock*, I participated in SAR tactics development and planning, which included soliciting the support of the hill tribesmen in Laos. SAR tactics had been on my mind for some time, and we had expended considerable effort on training in this area prior to the cruise. We certainly weren't the greatest experts, but we were more knowledgeable than the other units on *Yankee Station* during that first year of flying up north.'

Smith assisted in the first night rescue attempt in enemy territory on 6-7 November – an extensive effort to retrieve an F-105 pilot near Phu Ban, 25 miles south of Nam Dinh. Two USAF A-1Es were lost and their pilots captured during the course of the mission. A USAF CH-3C with a crew of four also was shot down, and one of its parajumpers was retrieved by an SH-3A from HS-2, embarked in USS *Independence* (CVA-62).

'I had just returned from a successful road recce mission', Cdr Smith explained. 'As I was finishing my debriefing, it was reported that someone had picked up two beepers 15 miles south of Hanoi. After studying the maps, I requested that we immediately launch a SAR CAP, but the request was refused on the basis that it was within two hours of sunset, and by the time we got on scene it would be dark. I appealed, arguing that if we waited until dawn there could be no rescue in view of the presumed number of enemy personnel and defences in the area. With reluctance, I was finally granted approval to go have a "look-see" and report back. I was advised that the E-1B radar aeroplane would be up on "Middleman" (circuit) so that we could talk directly with the ship and/or CTF-77.

'So, with my wingman, Lt Gary Gottschalk, we launched and headed to the scene, arriving at early dusk. We made a number of passes over the area but could not raise hide nor hair of any beeper, although we did draw some 37 mm fire from three locations. By now it was pretty dark, and from our relatively low altitude the muzzle flashes from the AAA batteries really stood out. In spite of our seeming lack of success, we weren't yet ready to give up.

'The terrain to the south and southwest of Hanoi is characterised by a low flat plain, which then gives way to some karst outcroppings leading to sharp hills rising to several thousand feet. We had been searching at the edge of the flat plain, and decided to move our efforts into the base of the hills. I knew the area fairly well, but two of the 37mm sites were new to me, and weren't on my map plot. As we moved our search five to ten miles further west, we suddenly

heard an intermittent beeper, but could not get a direction on it. We had now been airborne for about four hours, and I was beginning to be concerned about our fuel if we had to stay considerably longer, although we had enough for another hour or so on station.

'As we went back and forth, it seemed that we could receive the beeper in only a narrow cone to the northwest of the downed airman. Apparently, he was in a niche in the karst, and the terrain blocked out the transmissions except in one direction. I wanted to get a helicopter in there, but we certainly needed a better location first. I tried to make voice contact on his survival radio but to no avail. We could hear him try to transmit, but all we were receiving was a "rasping" noise. Apparently, he could hear us but we couldn't hear him. I asked him if he had a flashlight. Nothing in response. I asked him several other things – I don't remember what – and finally I mentioned a cigarette lighter. I told him that I was going to make a run on where I thought he was, and when I came close he was to light the lighter. I did, and he did, and there he was off to our left.

'We called to get a helicopter in there, and I was surprised that the response was immediately in the affirmative. We then had to bide our time and worry about our fuel, which by then was running rather low.

'After waiting only 35 minutes, we got a call from the helicopter off the SAR destroyer reporting that he was on his way in. I was expecting that he would be escorted in, and was somewhat surprised to see that he was alone. The problem now was how to put the helicopter on the right spot, since it was difficult to pick out detailed ground features because of the darkness. Gary got the helicopter in position, and I told him that I would come by, flash my lights, make a run and turn on my lights as soon as I was over the survivor. The helo driver was concerned about whether he'd be able to see the guy, so I told him he'd be the one with the cigarette lighter.

'The whole thing went better than expected, with one exception. As I was pulling up from my run I got a lot lower than I wanted, and I found myself face to face with the top of a tree. I clipped some branches, but except for scaring the hell out of me, it didn't do any damage, other than to my ego. I didn't say a word. I looked back and was finally able to pick up the helicopter heading in. I pulled up and, after turning on my lights, made two runs on the AAA sites. They started firing, and it apparently

Two A-1Hs from VA-152 prepare for launch from *Oriskany* in 1965. This photograph clearly shows the typical markings layout for US Navy Skyraiders of the era. The carrier and squadron designation were applied above and below, respectively, the NAVY titling. The last five digits of the six-digit Bureau Number were applied in large numerals on the tail below the carrier air wing tail code (AH for CVW-16). The type designation A-1H and the full bureau number were applied in small letters below the horizontal stabiliser. The last two digits of the nose number, or modex, were applied in small numbers at the tip of the rudder. The rotating beacon at the top of the vertical stabiliser can be used as a date marker for Skyraiders, as they were progressively installed on A-1s in the 1965-early 1966 timeframe. BuNo 137502 was supplied to the VNAF following the completion of its service with the US Navy (*Gary Gottschalk via Wayne Mutza collection*)

worked, for they didn't fire at the helicopter at all. I must have lucked out and got a bunch of amateurs, because they didn't come close to me either.

'About then the helicopter pilot called and said that he had the survivor and was heading back out. I had intended that we would escort the helicopter to the beach, but just then we heard another beeper. It seems that there were two beepers on simultaneously, which probably explains why we weren't able to previously get a homing bearing. We now had our work cut out for us.

VA-152 A-1H BuNo 134518 presents a warlike pose en route to a target in Southeast Asia in 1965. This 'Wild Ace' 'Spad' is armed with two 1000-lb Mk 83 and four 500-lb bombs. (*Gary Gottschalk via Wayne Mutza collection*)

'There was at least one more downed airman here, and we needed to locate him soon while we still had some fuel left. This second guy was much easier to pinpoint than the first one, since we were able to home in on his beeper. Additionally, we were able to establish voice communications with him, and he gave us directions as we closed in on him. I finally located him in a crevice at the base of a large karst outcropping.

'We contacted the powers that be and explained the situation as best we could. We advised that we needed a relief, and recommended that there be a visual hand off through the night so that he could be picked up at first light. We were first told that relief would be on scene in about an hour, which to us was totally unsatisfactory. We pleaded to get someone there IMMEDIATELY. In reply we got the standard "Wait, Out", but shortly thereafter were advised that relief was on the way.

'At that point I figured that if we left within the next few minutes, we had barely enough fuel to get back to the ship. I concluded that Gary had a bit more than I did because I'd wasted a lot tooling around making runs. Nevertheless, it was clear that both of us were in trouble. I advised the ship that, if necessary, I'd remain on scene until I could effect a visual hand off, and if I didn't have enough fuel I'd ditch in Brandon Bay. Suddenly, Adm Ralph Cousins came on the horn, identified himself and directed that I

Cdr Gordon H Smith was executive officer of VA-152 during the 'Wild Aces'' first war deployment in Southeast Asia. Smith, who would command the squadron during its second combat cruise, was highly regarded by his unit. He went on to become a rear admiral (*Gary Gottschalk via Wayne Mutza collection*)

head home NOW. I responded that he was cutting out, that I was transmitting blind, and that I intended to wait for relief.

'Shortly thereafter two F-4s suddenly appeared. I immediately directed Gary to head home, and proceeded to try to show the Phantom IIs where the guy was. It was a bit frustrating because I couldn't get them to come down low enough to show them much. However, I finally got them to see me, and I made a run marking "on top" by turning my lights on. Of course this immediately drew some fire, which

startled the F-4 drivers, but by now I was used to it. As before, the shooters were lousy shots, and I don't believe that they came very close.

'As I headed home, I was resigned to the fact that I was going to have to ditch, and was preparing myself, both mentally and physically, for that event. I tightened my shoulder straps to the point that it hurt. Suddenly, I picked up the ship's TACAN (TACtical Air Navigation) and couldn't believe what I was seeing because the carrier was 20 degrees to the right and 40 miles closer than I thought it would be. This just couldn't be, but I wasn't going to argue about it, except for a while I was convinced that there was something wrong with my TACAN. Finally, the ship confirmed my position and I figured that I had a good chance of making it.

'About 30 miles out I ran headlong into a small thunderstorm and got buffeted around quite a bit. Again I was having some doubts since I didn't know when I would come out of the clouds. However, once these cleared, there was the ship seven miles ahead of me. The LSO (Landing Signal Officer) came up on the radio and told me that we wouldn't change frequencies, and to call the ball. I came back with "507 Ball. State Zero". His calm response was "Roger Ball, Roger Zero". I landed without any fuss.

'Following my debriefing by the LSO, he told me that he thought there was something wrong with my engine, and I should have it checked, because there weren't the usual orange-yellow flames coming from my exhaust stacks – just some faint blue ones. I thanked him but didn't say another word, for I knew what had happened. I had landed with my mixture almost all the way back in manual lean – so much for check-off lists!

'I figured that I was in trouble, and that was confirmed in the mission debrief. First, I was just the XO, and my skipper was furious that I'd risked another of his A-1s. But in all fairness, at that point he didn't know the whole story. Then I was told that the other carrier group commander wanted my head for "disobedience of a lawful order". I had a private session with Adm Cousins, and after that I felt much better. My best support came from *Oriskany's* skipper, Capt Bart Connelly. He had always been a strong supporter and good friend, but it was to be 30 years before I would know the full story, and the details of what he did for me that night.

'I solicited his help and influence to get us on a pre-dawn launch to go in and pick up the other guy. At this point I was feeling pretty good about everything. If we had waited until the next day to commence the rescues it would have been midday before we got everything set up to pick them up, and in view of the environment, that would have been too late.

'*Oriskany's* flying cycle ran from noon to midnight, and the fact that we returned after midnight screwed everything up by delaying the re-spot of the deck and preparations for the next day's cycle. Now I was asking that we conduct a launch out of sequence in the middle of our down period. On the other hand, I had first-hand knowledge of the on-scene situation, the location of the downed airman, the terrain and the location of the air defences. I believed that if we could go in and do a quick "snatch", we stood a better than even chance of being successful. If we took four hours to sort things out in the morning, our chances would be nil.

'Now begins the exciting part. I had "Gordie" Wileen as my wingman, and we were airborne about 1.5 hours before sunrise. We picked up the SH-3A at a prearranged rendezvous and proceeded to the target area. The trip in from the beach was uneventful. The weather was hazy, and we were

An A-1J from VA-152 launches two five-inch rockets at a target just off the North Vietnamese coast in 1965. Rockets were used extensively by US Navy 'Spads' for flak suppression, close air support, attacking patrol boats and water-borne logistic craft and covering downed air crews during SAR/RESCAP missions (*US Navy/Lt J M Watson III*)

over an undercast, which was typical around dawn in that part of the world. The clouds had settled in the valleys, with some of the hills protruding above the tops. It took me a while to get oriented, but once I did, I was able to visualise the terrain below the clouds in detail.

'As it started to get light, some breaks in the clouds began to appear. I had parked the helicopter over a ridgeline, where I felt confident that he was relatively safe. "Gordie" was babysitting it, and I advised him not to go any further to the northwest. I then proceeded to find a hole in the clouds in order to get below and scout out the situation. As I approached the downed airman at low altitude, his beeper came on. I then felt confident that we could pick him up as soon as the clouds broke up a bit more. At the same time it occurred to me that it was possible that the guy had already been captured, and that the enemy were using his beeper to set up a trap. This had happened on two other occasions that I knew of. However, I quickly put that idea aside and focused on positive thoughts.

'I was drawing a lot of 37 mm fire, and it appeared that the bad guys had brought in the first team, because they were far more accurate than the night before. I got out of there and set up a plan whereby "Gordie" and I would make runs on the AAA sites in coordination with the helo coming in for the pick-up. I would have to give him a verbal picture of the location of things below because I didn't want to take the time to do it visually once the clouds broke up enough for him to see for himself.

'As I popped up through the clouds, I looked for the helicopter and he wasn't where he was supposed to be. I looked to my right and there he was, just where I didn't want him. I screamed on the radio for him to move to the southeast NOW!!! As he started to turn, the bad guys opened up and everything started to fall apart quickly. The helicopter pilot announced that he'd been hit, and I immediately saw that he was streaming fuel – and a lot of it. He stated that he would continue to the southeast as the best and safest way to the water, and I concurred.

'I was starting to tell the rest of the world what was happening when "Gordie" calmly announced that he was hit and on fire. He was behind me, and when I turned I could see him trailing a lot of smoke, but no flames. Now we had a helluva situation on our hands. I told him to head straight out and not wait for us. I had to do a lot of "S" turning to stay with the slower helicopter, and "Gordie" needed to get over water ASAP.

'After considerable conversation over the next several minutes, the helicopter driver concluded that he was losing fuel at almost 200 lbs a minute. It didn't take a mathematical genius to figure that he probably didn't have enough to get beyond the beach. If he was to take the shortest route to the water we would have to cut across the southern part of the Red River valley, and if we continued slightly to the right of our present heading it would take us right across Than Hoa. Either way, we would have been extremely vulnerable. So I told him to turn right to a heading of 240 degrees. Of course he thought I'd gone completely insane, but we finally talked it out. Besides, I told him to "Trust me" – and he did.

About 35 miles ahead was a 5500-ft hill, which I think is the tallest point in North Vietnam. The top is barren, and it is extremely remote. I'd often thought that if I ever found myself on the ground in that region, that's where I'd want to be. I figured that it would take days for the bad guy to get there. As the countryside got more remote, the helicopter was losing fuel at a faster rate than we previously thought, and it was going to be very tight. At that point I was glad that we took the course we did. We finally made it and the SH-3A sat down on the very top of the hill, but with little fuel remaining. I congratulated the crew on getting down in one piece, and told them that we should have someone to pick them up within an hour. The response was "We trusted you so far, didn't we?"'

The Sea King crew was duly rescued by a US Navy UH-2 and a USAF HH-3E. By this time, the three remaining USAF CH-3C crewmen that had been downed the previous day had been captured. Smith continued;

'Along the way, I'd kept in continuous radio contact with "Gordie", as well as with the SAR destroyer east of Brandon Bay. His A-1 experienced a complete hydraulic failure and the underfuselage had been badly damaged, preventing him from extending his landing gear. "Gordie" was going to proceed to Da Nang and land gear up. The SAR destroyer had a helicopter on the way, with an escort, to pick up the downed crewmen on Hill 5500. I didn't have anything to do, so I had a message relayed to *Oriskany* that I was proceeding to Da Nang and would return to the ship later.

'I sorely wanted to see what we could do to go back and get that poor bastard we'd left in that karst 18 miles from Hanoi. It was clear though that we'd never get approval to mount another effort under the circumstances. Besides, I was getting tired, and it was showing. I hadn't had any sleep in the last 30 hours, and I'd been airborne more than 15 of the last 22. The adrenalin rush was gone, and I was having a sinking spell.

'When I finally got to Da Nang, "Gordie" was still orbiting, waiting for them to prepare the field for his wheels up landing. He had the situation well in hand and didn't need my help, so I went ahead and landed. I watched him come in and everything was perfect – a real professional job. After giving "Gordie" a hug and downing four cups of coffee, I returned to the ship. Another day in the Tonkin Gulf.

'It was not until 30 years later that I discovered why *Oriskany* was in so close to the beach when I returned that night. Capt Connelly had been following my situation closely, and had decided to help out a bit. He cleared the bridge of all personnel except for himself and the officer of

VA-152's Lt Gordon Wileen walked away from this gear-up landing of A-1H BuNo 134563 at Da Nang in November 1965. He had diverted in his 'Spad' to Da Nang after taking hits from enemy fire during a rescue mission in North Vietnam (*USAF via Wayne Mutza collection*)

A Skyraider from VA-152 makes a rocket-firing run against an AAA site near Cape Bang in 1965. Note the lack of a bridge at the intersection of the roads on either side of the river – this had been destroyed some time earlier by CVW-16. Action photos such as this one of US Navy A-1s are rare because the wingmen with the cameras were also kept busy dodging enemy fire whilst over the target area (*US Navy/Lt J M Watson III via Wayne Mutza collection*)

Lt Gordon Wileen, in dress blue uniform, poses in front of pristine VA-152 A-1H BuNo 137502 AH 587 in March 1966 during the brief respite between the squadron's first and second Vietnam deployments. Note the mission markings beneath the cockpit. Lt E D 'Bud' Edson is strapped into the idling 'Spad' (*Gary Gottschalk via Wayne Mutza collection*)

the deck, Lt(jg) Bruce Bell, and headed west in violations of all the rules. He wanted no witnesses, and he swore Bell to secrecy. There is no question that without Connelly's aggressive action I would not have made it back that night.'

Cdr Smith was awarded the Silver Star for his actions during the SAR mission. 'As I recall, our truly fearless and brilliant XO Cdr Gordon Smith was awarded seven Silver Stars for the combined 1965-66 deployments, all for RESCAP missions in which he participated', explained Gordon Wileen. Smith later rose to the rank of rear admiral.

VA-152 lost an A-1H on 9 November when Lt Cdr Paul Merchant's aircraft (BuNo 137566) was hit in the engine by AAA during a night attack on trucks 35 miles southeast of Vinh. Merchant nursed the 'Spad' over the beach, but his engine failed and he ditched off the coast. He was rescued by a US Navy helicopter as two enemy boats approached him.

Four days later, Lt Clarke was forced to make a gear-up landing at Da Nang after taking hits from AAA during a SAR mission. VA-152 CO Cdr Knutson continued the unsuccessful SAR effort while taking 26 hits to his Skyraider, for which he was awarded the Silver Star.

On 17 November, a VA-152 A-1H (BuNo 135244) flown by CVW-16 staff operations officer Lt Cdr Jesse J Taylor Jr was lost during an Alpha strike on the Hai Dong Bridge east of Hanoi. Taylor, who had volunteered to fly the mission, and Lt Cdr Eric H Schade, were participating in a SAR effort for a VA-163 A-4E pilot downed during the raid (one of three US Navy jets to be lost on the bridge strike). The A-1 was hit in the port wing by AAA as Taylor flew low trying to locate the pilot, and although he managed to clear the target area, he was killed when the Skyraider crashed 15 miles southwest of Haiphong. Taylor's remains were returned in December 1975. Posthumously awarded the Navy Cross, he became the namesake for the frigate USS *Taylor* (FFG-50).

Schade's A-1 was also hit by AAA, and its pilot landed heavily on his return to CVA-34. Having suffered further damage, it never flew again.

By the time *Oriskany* returned to Alameda on 16 December 1965, CVW-16 had lost no fewer than 52 aircraft (including damage write-offs and mishaps) and 19 pilots. 'VA-152 lost 13 "Spads". We deployed with 12', Gordon Wileen recalled, counting the A-1s that were written off for battle damage. 'We were continually going to Cubi Point for replacement aircraft'.

# 'MAIN BATTERY', 'MAPE'S APES', 'ARABS' AND OWLS'

VA-196 'Main Battery' had been preparing for a 'good will' cruise to the Mediterranean in 1965, but the unit, led by Cdr Joseph Gallagher, found itself heading for the South China Sea when *Bon Homme Richard* sailed from Alameda on 21 April 1965. The unit would ultimately fly 2173 combat sorties over North and South Vietnam, dropping more than 7,000,000 lbs of ordnance.

The deployment cost the squadron four A-1s and three pilots. Lt Cdr James T Kearns was killed on 14 September 1965 when his A-1J (BuNo 142057) was destroyed in the premature explosion of its own bomb during a mission five miles southwest of Soc Trang, in South Vietnam. Ten days later, Cdr Gallagher baled out after his A-1H (BuNo 135274) was hit by small arms fire whilst returning to CVA-31 from an administrative visit to Chu Lai – he was recovered by a Marine Corps helicopter.

While flying an armed reconnaissance mission on 28 September along a railway line near Qui Vinh, north of the DMZ, the A-1H (BuNo 134482) of Lt Cdr Carl J Woods was hit by AAA. He flew his 'Spad' more than 40 miles to the Tonkin Gulf and baled out of the burning aircraft off the coast. Although a USAF SAR helicopter was soon on the scene, the pilot was found to be dead. Woods had almost certainly drowned.

Finally, on 2 December 1965, during an armed reconnaissance mission 35 miles north of Dong Hoi, Lt Cdr Gerald R Roberts (in A-1H BuNo 139755) was lost on his third run on a bridge either to AAA or by flying into the ground. His remains were recovered in 1993-94.

VA-196's last 'Spad' deployment ended on 13 January 1966, when the unit returned to Lemoore. It was transferred to Oceana two months later, whereupon it commenced transitioning to the A-6A Intruder.

VA-52 'Knightriders' deployed on its second combat tour of Southeast Asia, again with CVW-5, on board *Ticonderoga* on 28 September 1965. Commencing operations on 5 November, the unit lost two aircraft in short order to mishaps. An A-1H

The pilot of VA-52 A-1H BuNo 139645 escorts a USAF HU-16B amphibian on a RESCAP mission over the Tonkin Gulf in 1966. VA-52 returned to Vietnam on board *Ticonderoga* (CVA-14) with CVW-5. This aircraft is armed with four 19-shot pods of 2.75-in rockets and Mk 24 flares (*Tom Hansen via Wayne Mutza collection*)

(BuNo 137590) suffered an hydraulic failure due to oil starvation whilst returning from a mission on 16 November – the pilot was rescued after ditching. Another engine failure brought down a second A-1H (BuNo 137621) that had been launched as a RESCAP for a raid on Hai Duong on 1 December. Its pilot was also plucked from the sea.

Cdr John C Mape relieved Cdr Lee T McAdams as CO on 10 December 1965, and so began a tragically short period when the 'Knightriders' were known as 'Mape's Apes'. On 3 January 1966, a section of Skyraiders attacked a VC troop concentration ten miles north of Saigon. Lt J W Donahue's A-1J (BuNo 142081 – the last Skyraider ever built) was hit by small arms fire during his ninth pass on the target. Despite his aircraft being on fire, Donahue nursed it ten miles away from the target area before crash-landing. He was was rescued by a US Army helicopter.

On 13 April, while a section of VA-52 Skyraiders was flying an armed reconnaissance mission 15 miles south of Vinh, an SA-2 was fired at the A-1s. Cdr Mape's A-1H (BuNo 139692) was destroyed in a fireball, the aircraft having become the first US Navy 'Spad' to be downed by a SAM. XO Cdr Robert R Worchesek became the new commanding officer three days later. Mape's remains were recovered by a JTF-FA team in 1994.

The unit lost its last aircraft on 18 April when, during a SAR mission for a downed A-1H from VA-115, the A-1J (BuNo 142032) flown by Lt A D Wilson was hit by automatic weapons fire on its fifth run on Tiger Island, just off the coast from the DMZ. Wilson ditched offshore and was rescued by a USAF helicopter. CVA-14 finished its final line period 48 hours later and returned to Alameda on 13 May 1966.

## 'ARABS' TO THE RESCUE

The 'Arabs' of VA-115, lead by Cdr M C Cook, arrived in the Tonkin Gulf in October 1965 with CVW-11 on board CVA-63. The deployment was unique in two respects. Firstly, it was to be the only one in which a carrier air wing included both A-1 and A-6 attack units (VA-85), and secondly, experimental camouflage was applied to US Navy 'Spads'.

During the eight-month deployment, VA-115 flew 2051 combat sorties and dropped 6.9 million pounds of ordnance on targets in North and South Vietnam during armed reconnaissance, close air support and RESCAP missions. Lt Cdr Jerry Tabrum recalled a SAR mission he participated in on 14 March 1966;

'We had been on station for about two hours, flying a ten-mile-long racetrack pattern over the Tonkin Gulf, when we heard the Mayday call on the guard channel. A USAF F-4C had been hit by AAA and the two-man crew had ejected over water between the North Vietnamese coast and Hon Me Island.

'We arrived at the site of the downed flyers in about 12 minutes. After spotting them, an HU-16 made a nice water landing and taxied

VA-115 A-1J BuNo 142016 taxis forward on the flightdeck of *Kitty Hawk* on 5 May 1966 as the arresting gear cross-deck pendant retracts. This aircraft was one of several VA-115 Skyraiders that featured experimental water-based paint camouflage applied to its uppersurfaces for the duration of the deployment. The green and olive scheme was abandoned after the cruise. This aircraft was also eventually passed onto the VNAF (*US Navy via Robert L Lawson collection*)

This VA-115 Skyraider recovered at Da Nang AB after receiving damage to its starboard wing during a combat mission over Southeast Asia. The A-1's rugged construction enabled many shot up aircraft to reach safety. However, a good number of these machines were written off once the damage they had suffered was assessed as being beyond economical repair (*USAF via Robert F Dorr collection*)

Another of VA-115's camouflaged A-1Hs taxis toward a catapult on board *Kitty Hawk*. The black modex '503' is outlined in white for increased visibility. This A-1H (BuNo 135263) is armed with four M117 750-lb low-drag bombs on the outboard wing pylons and 1000-lb low-drag bombs on the two inboard stations (*US Navy via Wayne Mutza collection*)

toward the survivors. We scanned the general area for water traffic, but there was only one vessel – a junk, one mile north that was heading away from the site at best speed. The HU-16 began the task of picking up the F-4 crew. At this point, I noticed a splash in the water 200 yards west of the site. "Did you release something", I asked my wingman, Lt Cdr Manny Benero. "Negative", he replied.

'We both saw the second splash. This one was 75 yards east of the HU-16. Ten seconds later the right wing of the Albatross exploded in orange flame and dense black smoke. I looked westward toward the beach and saw numerous muzzle flashes. We commenced making rocket runs on the beach using our five-inch High Velocity Aircraft Rockets (HVARs). After depleting them, we strafed the area with our 20 mm cannons. This seemed to halt the mortar fire for the time being.

'Benero assumed the duties of the SAR on-scene commander, and made an immediate request for rescue helicopters for the two F-4 flyers and the Albatross crew. Meanwhile, the North Vietnamese despatched three small boats from shore in an effort to capture the survivors. I made a rocket run on the vessels with two pods of 2.75-in FFARs, each pod containing 19 rockets. I fired them at the boats and they soon disappeared.

'We remained over the burning HU-16, eventually vectoring in two SH-3s from HS-4, embarked in USS *Yorktown* (CVS-10). Despite taking fire, the Sea Kings rescued five survivors before being forced to leave.

'By this time, a very low overcast had come in from seaward, forcing us to stay at a very altitude in order to remain in visual contact with the Albatross. The final crewman was rescued by a UH-2 vectored in from USS *England* (DLG-22), terminating the two-and-a-half-hour ordeal.

'Two crewmen from the HU-16 had been killed by the direct hit on their aircraft. The four remaining crew, plus the F-4C crew, survived.'

VA-115 lost only two 'Spads' to enemy action during its first Vietnam combat deployment, which ended in June 1966. On 1 February, Lt(jg) B S Eakin's A-1J (BuNo 142038) caught fire after receiving a hit over Ban Senphan, in Laos – he baled out and was rescued. On 17 April Lt(jg) William L Tromp was lost during a night coastal armed reconnaissance mission between Mu Ron Ma and Vinh. Tromp (in A-1H BuNo 135398) attacked a water-borne logistics craft in the mouth of the Song Gia Hoi River. He then told his wingman to abort

VA-115's A-1H BuNo 139778 'Arab 506' awaits overhaul in CONUS following the unit's sole Vietnam deployment embarked in *Kitty Hawk*. The experimental camouflage paint has largely worn off, revealing the original markings underneath. Once refurbished, this aircraft was also supplied to the VNAF (*US Navy via Wayne Mutza collection*)

his run because a SAM had been launched at Tromp's aircraft during his attack. As both A-1s headed out to sea, Tromp radioed that he had an emergency, after which all contact was lost. US divers subsequently located the wreck of his aircraft in 1973, but no remains were found. Indeed, the North Vietnamese reported that he died in captivity.

The squadron also lost two Skyraiders in operational mishaps, the first on 11 March when a catapult launch bridle failed and the A-1J (BuNo 142071) rolled off the deck and into the sea – the unnamed pilot survived. A launch incident also occurred on 19 May when an A-1J (BuNo 142051) experienced engine failure during its catapult stroke off the bow of CVA-63. Again, the unnamed pilot was rescued.

## TRAIL INTERDICTION

VA-215 'Barn Owls', led by Cdr Robert C Hessom, returned to the war zone with CVW-21 on board *Hancock* in early December 1965, having finished its first combat cruise aboard CVA-19 just six months earlier. CVW-21 focused on operations in South Vietnam, flying support missions over the Mekong Delta for the Marines during Operations *Jackstay* and *Deckhouse*. Thereafter, *Hancock* headed north for *Yankee Station*.

Capt (then Cdr) George Carlton, who was XO of the 'Barn Owls', described his squadron's work over the Ho Chi Minh Trail;

'War material was transported from North Vietnam to the VC in South Vietnam along the Ho Chi Minh Trail (HCMT). This multi-trailed route started at the Mu Gia pass, some 50 miles north of the DMZ, and meandered south over 400 miles through Laos and Cambodia, before ending near An Loc, in South Vietnam. Throughout its entire length, the trail was never more than 10-15 miles from Vietnam's western border. Therefore, it provided the enemy with the opportunity to move material across the boarder into Vietnam at numerous well-concealed and varying points of entry. The HCMT was heavily forested throughout its entire length, affording its users protection against aerial observation. Thus, the material of war was moved along the trail almost at will.

'North of Mu Gia pass, the USAF had priority in a zone called Route Package I (RP I), which ran from the DMZ northward for about 60 miles.

North from there, the US Navy presided over Route Package II (RP II), which continued north another 40 miles to just south of Vinh.

'Most war material arrived in North Vietnam through the port of Haiphong, with the remainder coming in on the northeast rail link with China. Under our political Rules of Engagement (RoE), the most worth-while target in North Vietnam lay untouched. Haiphong docks, eminently lucrative as a strategic choke point, were never hit. Thus, tactical aircraft were given the task of interdicting the movement of war materials as they headed south in trucks, wagons, carts, backpacks etc.

'In my tours with VA-215 in 1966-67, our interdiction efforts were largely confined to RP II and along the HCMT from the Mu Gia pass south through Laos. Our missions into RP II were always at night. The concentrations of AAA along RP I (the main route south from Vinh) were considered formidable, and most of the traffic south occurred during the hours of darkness anyway. Thus, we went in at night – usually in flights of four – choosing route segments with minimal AAA cover. Each Skyraider carried four high intensity parachute flares, 800 rounds of 20 mm ammo, two 19-shot 2.75-in rocket packs and a mix of four 250- and 500-lb bombs. Having no onboard radar, infrared or night vision aids, we were limited to our "Mark One" eyeballs for searching and tracking.

'Tactically, we would split the lead section, with one aeroplane flying along a tract offset a few hundred yards to one side of the route while the No 2 bird flew, slightly in trail, along the other side. We flew at a few hundred feet AGL (Above Ground Level) at around 165 knots, typically from south to north, on dark, moonless nights, as often their trucks, heading south, would have dim-running lights on under those conditions. Visibility was a bit better through the side canopy, as looking forward through the windshield, covered with a thick bullet proof material, and through the propeller as well, restricted vision somewhat.

'The second section – "birds" Nos 3 and 4 – would trail along at 3000 ft, ready to illuminate the scene with flares at the call of the flight leader. On sighting a potential target, the flight leader called for flares. No 3 A-1 would drop first, while No 4 climbed to 5000 ft for the first run. Mean-while, No 1, with No 2 in trail, climbed, ready to dive in behind No 4.

'It was a difficult cat and mouse game at best, for at the first indication of our presence, the trucks cut their lights and headed for cover in ditches and under trees. Flying from blackness into the bright light of the flares, and then from the light back into the blackness on pull-up, induced vertigo. On moonlit nights, we often worked without flares. This provided more surprise, but often proved frustrating, as targets spotted through the side canopy at low altitude could be lost in the attack while looking through the windshield, the propeller and the dimly lit gunsight.

'While we did nail some trucks from time to time, the Skyraider was simply not equipped for that mission. It proved to be a huge expenditure with little reward.

'We worked the HCMT south from Mu Gia pass both day and night, although by mid-1966 the pass itself was off limits. Being a choke point, it was infested with AAA. Because of the difficulties in seeing anything moving along the trail from the air through the intense jungle growth, sometimes layered over with several canopies, we often worked with USAF FACs flying O-1 Bird Dogs. Bombs were the preferred weapons.

Nine of VA-215's Skyraiders occupy *Hancock's* aft flightdeck on 15 June 1966, in company with CVW-5's F-8E Crusaders, RF-8G Photo-Crusader, A-4C and A-4E Skyhawks and E-1B Tracers. The US Navy's ability to conduct intensive combat flight operations from small-deck carriers such as this one with modern aircraft was a tribute to the skill of its pilots and the vessel's various Air Departments (*US Navy/PHC J McClure*)

'The FACs would mark the aim points with "Willie Peter" (white phosphorus) smoke rockets, and we would drop bombs on the smoke. The FAC, armed with the latest intelligence on trail concentrations and movements, would have us drop a few bombs at a time, probing for secondary explosions. Failing this, he would move on to other spots, marking each one with smoke rockets. Usually carrying eight or more bombs each, we could probe several targets. More often than not the results were disappointing. We jokingly referred to these missions as making tooth picks the hard way.

'On one occasion, working just south of Tchepone, in Laos, we cooked off the biggest and most prolonged series of secondary explosions that I witnessed in my two tours in Southeast Asia. The FAC had just marked a new target, and I led the first three A-1s down an east-west line into the target, dropping one 500-pounder each. As I was pulling out and circling back for another go, I observed No 4 well off our dive line, heading northwest. I radioed, "Don't drop No 4 – you're way off target", just as he released his bomb.

'Well, his errant bomb started a series of secondary explosions that lasted a full eight to ten minutes – an ammo dump, we speculated during the debrief. I advised the FAC that we were ready to drop more bombs around that area, but he called us off. The hot target was unauthorised! We then proceeded to expend the rest of our bombs on his smoke signals, with no discernible results. Such were the restraints of the political RoE.

'The No 4 "Barn Owl", a nugget (a relatively new pilot), had somehow gotten disoriented during the roll-in on that fortuitous drop. I was certainly pleased with the results, but could hardly condone the error. Back on the carrier, I was queried, somewhat tongue-in-cheek, as to whether or not the nugget should be written up for an award. I replied that he might better be awarded with time in hack (disciplinary status)!

'Our infrequent night missions along the HCMT were in support of USAF AC-47 and AC-130 gunships. These aircraft were especially configured with waist gunners, infrared sensors and night vision scopes. Essentially, we rode shotgun on them, usually in trail at 5000 ft AGL. They also carried parachute flares that were used to illuminate the scene.

'Typically, on making contact, they would drop flares and call us in to expend our bombs while they were making a 180-degree turn back to the scene to get into position for their gunners to rake the area. It all required close coordination, and often resulted in a melee as we made our runs while they were off target turning around – all without running lights.

'Later, the USAF developed tactics using two gunships, one trailing the other, which resulted in them being able to keep fire directed at the target almost continuously. We did cook off some secondary explosions, but, all in all, finding transport vehicles moving along jungle trails at night was difficult at best, and roundly ineffective in the overall scheme of things.'

George Carlton also participated in a mission involving four 'Barn Owl' A-1s on a pre-briefed mission over Laos in the spring of 1966;

'We were each loaded with full 20 mm ammo, four 500-lb bombs, 300 gallons of 115/145 high octane Avgas in the centreline drop tank and full internal fuel (360 gallons). This was a relatively light load for the A-1, allowing us six to eight hours of mission time. We were catapulted from *Hancock* on *Yankee Station*, 125 miles east of the DMZ, at 1000 hrs and then headed to a coast-in point south of the DMZ. Arriving a few miles north of Tchepone by 1130 hrs, we received a hot reception from what I took to be a 37 mm AAA battery. We were at 6500 ft, and as I ordered the flight to break hard right, the fire fell short and below us.

'I cursed myself for not giving Tchepone (a known hot spot) a wider birth. By our RoE, we were forbidden from engaging in duels with AAA batteries not directly hindering our assigned mission. This was an example of a rule that I fully supported in that the risk/reward ratio was not favourable. But what *was* worth the risk?

'Our target that day, assigned by someone well up the chain-of-command, was a river ford (a place where a body of water can be crossed by wading) along the HCMT some 75-100 miles northwest of Tchepone. We arrived in the target area shortly after noon and easily found the river – actually a stream, no more than 50 ft across.

'From 6500 ft, I couldn't make out the ford, so I detached and dove down for a look, alerting the rest of the flight to be ready to suppress any ground fire that I might stir up. After a couple of passes up and down the stream, I found the ford, which looked to be rocks piled up in a band some eight to ten feet wide just below the water's surface. I gave the rest of the flight a mark-on-top and told them to start the drops, as I climbed back up for my run. Dropping strings of four each diagonally across the target, we took out the entire ford, including both approaches.

'As I looked over my shoulder on the climb out, I judged that the VC now had a nice swimming hole. I concluded further that it would probably take six to eight hours to construct a new ford displaced a few yards in either direction. The lack of hostile fire was probably an indication of how little the enemy valued this crossing.

'Setting a course for Tchepone, we settled back into a "loose deuce" formation – a holdover from World War 2 naval aviator Jimmy Thach's tactics – which gave good 360-degree surveillance around the flight. Remembering the reception that we had been afforded on passing Tchepone on the way in, I considered putting a few rounds of 20 mm into that

A VA-215 pilot starts the Wright R-3350 radial engine on the deck of *Hancock* in 1966. The powerful engine enabled the A-1 to carry the ordnance loads for which it is famous. The Battle Efficiency 'E' awarded to the squadron is displayed beneath the cockpit of this aircraft (*US Navy*)

pesky AAA sight, but discipline prevailed and we turned well north so as to avoid any temptation.

'I couldn't help thinking how the RoE were hamstringing our efforts in stopping the flow of material down the trail from north to south. Here we were hitting a stream ford, while vast concentrations of SAMs, ammo and fuel sat fully exposed on the docks at Haiphong, protected by a ten-mile circle into which we could not fly because of the RoE. "Theirs not to reason why, theirs but to do or die" – Tennyson's words came to mind.

'Under the strategy of the day, we were not allowed to interdict until the SAMs were in place and active, until the ammo and fuel had been reduced to small packets and loaded onto trucks, wagons, carts and bicycles, and until all was beyond ten miles and moving south under cover of darkness and dense jungle canopies. The absurdity of the situation seemed obvious, but as a squadron XO I assiduously avoided revealing my personal views in the presence of the junior pilots.

'Taking each mission as it came, I attempted to put the best possible face on any discussion of raison d'etre – should it come up.

'"Spads" flying west of Quang Tri. Do you hear me? This is 'Skylark', over."

'The transmission coming in over the guard channel broke my reverie like a thunderclap. "'Skylark', this is 'Barn Owl 1'. I'm in that vicinity", I responded.

'We soon established communications on another channel, and as it turned out "Skylark" was a USAF FAC flying an O-1 Bird Dog a few miles south of us. A flight of F-100s had just left him, low on fuel after a couple of passes. It seemed "Skylark" had what he described as a concentration of VC pinned down in some earthwork trenches and bunkers. I wished we still had the 16 500-pounders we had wasted on the ford. All we had left were our 20 mm cannons – some 3200 rounds. Maybe we could still be helpful.

'Setting up a racetrack pattern and spread out to keep continuous fire on the target, we started our runs using 35-degree dive angles. After my first pass, "Skylark" urged us to get steeper, advising that the trenches were narrow and very deep. We tried 60-degree runs – really steep for strafing. "Still not effective", he radioed.

'I said, "Okay, 'Barn Owls'. Let's take it upstairs and use the brakes". In 16 years of flying Skyraiders, I had never tried strafing from a 70-degree dive, but the A-1 was equipped with huge dive brakes designed to allow high angle dives while holding down speed, and thereby providing more time in the run, with increased accuracy resulting from lower release and pull-out altitudes. We set up to roll in above 10,000 ft, thus allowing ample time to establish a steady run at, or above, a 70-degree angle. Coming in at that angle to the target, the attitude of the aeroplane was between 90 and 110 degrees – pointed virtually straight down!

'The FAC was ecstatic. "Pour it on, 'Barn Owls!'" he urged. We made three or four 70-degree runs each, expending all our ammo – demonstrating once again the versatility and staying power of the magnificent Skyraider. As we collected ourselves, "Skylark" gave us a bomb-damage assessment of 25-30 killed in action.'

George Carlton also described a typical 'Spad' RESCAP mission. 'In support of SAR missions, the A-1s were especially well suited in that they alone had the staying power and low-altitude manoeuvrability to work in close support of the rescue vehicles – HU-16 amphibious aircraft for open sea missions and helicopters (flown from carriers, destroyers and cruisers) for both sea and overland missions.

'Typically, the A-1s carried full loads of 20 mm ammo (200 rounds for each of their four 20 mm cannons), two 19-shot 2.75-in rocket packs and a mix of two to four 250- and 500-lb bombs. I can also remember using napalm on one mission, but that was an exception, because the RoE would normally not allow it north of the DMZ. I was never involved with an HU-16 pick-up, but I spent many hours flying offshore in holding patterns with them awaiting any rescue situation to develop.

'Typically, after being relieved by the next RESCAP team, we had a free hour or so to search the coastline for water-borne logistics craft (WBLC), known colloquially as "wiblicks" – small boats or barges moving north or south along the coast, thus presumed to be involved in transporting war material. Almost without exception we could find something fitting that pattern. We learned to use caution when attacking these targets, as occasionally we came under fire from shore batteries while diving on the boats. We suspected that some were therefore being used as traps.'

VA-215's second Vietnam deployment was only slightly less costly than its first. Cdr Robert Hessom was killed on 5 March 1966 when his A-1H (BuNo 137589) crashed after flying 15 miles from where it had been hit by AAA south of Vinh during a *Rolling Thunder* strike. Cdr Frederick L Nelson duly assumed command. Hessom's remains were eventually recovered in 1994 near Ha Tinh.

Lt Cdr William P Egan was shot down (in A-1H BuNo 137576) by small arms fire whilst diving on a vehicle near Ban Senphan, in Laos, during a *Steel Tiger* armed reconnaissance mission on 29 April. No trace of him or his aircraft were ever found. Ten days later, Lt Cdr C W Sommers II was rescued by a US Navy helicopter 70 miles south of Cam Ranh Bay after he was forced to ditch his A-1H (BuNo 139616) during an anti-surface vessel patrol. Finally, The squadron lost an A-1J (BuNo 142050) on 14 May when it suffered a control system failure whilst being launched. The pilot was rescued by the plane guard UH-2 from HC-1 Det 1. VA-215 returned to Lemoore on 1 August 1966.

A-1H BuNo 135320 and A-1J BuNo 142039 are offloaded from the aircraft ferry USNS *Breton* (AKV-42) in March 1966 at NAS Cubi Point, Philippines, where such replacement aircraft were positioned as spares until needed. These Skyraiders would eventually replace 'Spads' lost or damaged over Southeast Asia. The aircraft have been sealed with 'Spraylat' to prevent corrosion during storage and transit. Cubi Point, and co-located Naval Station Subic Bay, were the main re-supply and repair bases for carriers and their air wings rotating in and out of the Tonkin Gulf during the Vietnam War. The base complex was a popular rest and recreation respite from the grind of daily air operations over Southeast Asia (*US Navy via W M Bowers*)

# ROUND TWO

The 'Swordsmen' of VA-145, led by Cdr H F Griffith, became the fourth A-1 unit to participate in their second war cruise with the Skyraider when CVW-14, this time embarked in *Ranger*, arrived on *Dixie Station* on 14 January 1966. With a temporary bombing halt then in effect north of the DMZ, the unit flew its first missions in support of US and ARVN forces in South Vietnam instead.

The end of the halt on 31 January brought a flurry of activity for the 'Swordsmen'. Griffith led a strike of six 'Spads' in adverse weather, and he and his wingman, Ens Walter S Bumgarner, destroyed two highway bridges and two staging areas. While turning away from the target area, Griffith received a SAR request to search for a VA-55 A-4 pilot downed near Dong Hoi. During the search, Griffith's A-1 was hit twice and rolled inverted. He emerged from the overcast still upside down, but managed to recover and proceed to a friendly airfield. Lt Cdr J Kenneth Hassett's section located the A-4 pilot offshore and covered the rescue.

The 'Swordsmen' suffered their first loss of the deployment the very next day, however. A four-aeroplane division was approaching its target near Ban Phathoung, in Laos, when it received a distress call from a VA-115 flight that was covering the scene over one of its downed pilots. Lt(jg) Eakin had baled out after being hit by AAA near Ben Senphan, also in Laos. The VA-145 division leader decided to complete his assigned mission and then go to the aid of the downed aviator.

Lt Dieter Dengler was the last to dive on the target, and his A-1J (BuNo 142031) was struck by ground fire as he rolled in. Dengler's Skyraider lost its wings when he hit trees crash-landing near the target area, and the pilot was soon captured by the Pathet Lao and imprisoned in Laos.

The son of a German soldier, Dengler endured months of torture and starvation before escaping with a handful of other Air America and USAF PoWs on 29 June. He was the only one to eventually be rescued on 20 July by USAF HH-3E. Emaciated, but joyous, after his gruelling experiences in captivity and on the run, Dengler was awarded the Navy Cross. His exploits have been featured in books, a documentary and a feature film over the past 30 years. Dieter Dengler succumbed to Lou Gehrig's disease on 7 February 2001.

On 10 February, Lt(jg) Gary D Hopps was killed when his A-1H (BuNo 137627) was hit by AAA and he slammed into the ground whilst diving on a bridge between

This photograph, taken on 2 February 1966 by an RA-5C Vigilante assigned to Reconnaissance Heavy Attack Squadron Nine, shows the wreckage of Lt(jg) Dieter Dengler's A-1J BuNo 142031 inside Laos. The fuselage lies on its port side, both wings have been sheared from the aircraft, the empennage has been broken off and the centreline external tank has been thrown a considerable distance to the right of the wreckage. Dengler, on his first combat mission with VA-145 on 1 February 1966, survived the shoot-down and crash-landing, but was captured by Pathet Lao forces. He escaped on 29 June 1966 and wandered in the jungle for three weeks before he was rescued (*US Navy*)

Having returned to duty after his rescue and transfer to Fleet Composite Squadron Seven as an A-4 Skyhawk pilot, Lt Dieter Dengler (right) flew his jet to Edwards Air Force Base, California, to meet the USAF Skyraider pilot who, by happenstance, spotted him in the North Vietnamese jungle on 20 July 1966 and called in a rescue helicopter. Col (Lt Col during the rescue) Eugene Deatrick (left) was commanding officer of the 1st Air Commando Squadron (*USAF/A1C Robert F Touboue via Robert F Door collection*)

Dong Hoi and the DMZ. Later that same day, Lt Kurt V Anderson destroyed another bridge with two direct hits. He and his wingman then conducted a road reconnaissance in mountainous terrain and came upon a truck convoy. Repeatedly attacking it with bombs, rockets and cannon fire, the two A-1 pilots destroyed four vehicles and damaged seven others.

On 25 February, Lt Cdr Clarence R Armstrong was escorting a reconnaissance aircraft off the coast of North Vietnam when, detecting a faint emergency beeper, he broke formation and descended through a solid overcast to 300 ft. Searching through fog and rain, he escorted a SAR helicopter to the scene. After rescuing a survivor, the helicopter crew learned that four more men remained in the water – they had ejected from a USAF RB-66C that had been damaged by an SA-2 near Vinh and eventually abandoned over the sea. Armstrong became on-scene commander, and supervised the rescue of the crewmen in the water.

In early March 1966, Lt Cdr John C Stovall and Lt(jg) David G Maples launched on a RESCAP patrol and were called in to search for a downed pilot through intense AAA and poor weather. Stovall detached Maples to locate and escort the rescue helicopter while he searched the area for the pilot. Both 'Swordsmen' took hits as they attacked enemy gun positions, but the rescue attempt was unsuccessful in locating the downed pilot.

On 10 March, XO Cdr Donald E Sparks and Lt(jg) Daniel P Farkas were diverted by weather from an armed reconnaissance mission over North Vietnam to a FAC over the A Shau Valley, in South Vietnam, where a larger enemy force had surrounded 100 US and ARVN special forces. Penetrating an 800-ft overcast concealing surrounding mountain peaks, Sparks and Farkas descended through a break in the clouds and bombed and strafed enemy forces through withering ground fire. They then climbed back up through the overcast before repeating their attack runs through the break. The pilots destroyed seven gun positions.

It was during this action that USAF Maj Bernard F Fisher landed his A-1E on the A Shau airstrip and rescued fellow 'Spad' pilot Maj D W 'Jump' Myers. Fisher was awarded the Medal of Honor for this action.

After a break from the war, *Ranger* returned to *Dixie Station* on 12 April. Thirteen days later, Lt(jg) Malcolm Johns experienced a rough-running engine and force-landed at Duc Hoa AB. On 26 April four 'Swordsmen' attacked a VC storage complex southeast of Saigon. Performing repeated attacks through intense small arms fire, they destroyed 25 large structures and damaged 15 others. A similar strike was flown two days later, destroying 35 structures and damaging 40 more.

*Ranger* arrived on *Yankee Station* on 29 April, and began a week of strike, armed reconnaissance and RESCAP missions. On 20 June, Lt Cdr John W Tunnell died when his A-1H (BuNo 139806) inexplicably crashed shortly after launching on a night strike mission.

Lt Thomas M Oprian and Lt(jg) Norman R Lessard enjoyed lively success on 26 June during a strike on a segment of Route IA. They interdicted the road at two points, put a bridge out of use, destroyed 15 trucks and caused a secondary explosion that sent a fireball 600 ft into the air.

The 'Swordsmen' welcomed Lt Dengler back aboard CVA-61 on 21 July after his escape and rescue. Sparks relieved Griffith as CO on 3 August, and two days later *Ranger* departed *Yankee Station*. The 3rd was marred by the loss of an A-1H (BuNo 134586), which had been hit by small arms fire during a road reconnaissance over North Vietnam. Coaxing his ailing aircraft back to *Ranger*, Lt(jg) David Franz suffered brake failure after landing and the A-1 rolled over the side of the carrier. The pilot was quickly recovered. When CVA-61 left for home, the 'Swordsmen' had flown 1700 combat missions and expended five million pounds of ordnance during 136 days on the line.

## 'CHAMPAGNE AIR WING'

The US Navy decided to alleviate the demanding schedule for its attack carriers by pressing anti-submarine warfare support aircraft carriers into service as limited attack carriers. USS *Intrepid* (CVS-11) was the first selected for this honor, deploying thrice to the Tonkin Gulf in that role.

On the first of these Vietnam deployments, *Intrepid* embarked CVW-10, known as the 'Champagne Air Wing', which included two A-4 units – VA-15 and VA-95 – and for the only time on a Vietnam-era carrier, two A-1H/J squadrons in the form of VA-165 'Boomers' and VA-176 'Thunderbolts'. After work-ups, *Intrepid* and CVW-10 departed Norfolk, Virginia, on 4 April 1966 and steamed to the Tonkin Gulf, via the Mediterranean and the Suez Canal, with 24 'Spads' embarked.

As *Intrepid* approached the war zone, the A-1 pilots incorporated knives and 9 mm sidearms as items of their survival equipment. The pilots attended JEST (Jungle Environmental Survival Training) at Cubi Point before CVS-11 took up its position at *Dixie Station*.

On 15 May 1966, VA-165 (led by Cdr Harry D Parode) and VA-176 (headed by Cdr Robert J Martin) launched their first strikes over South Vietnam from *Intrepid*. In two line periods of operations in II, III, and IV Corps areas, VA-176 flew almost 2000 combat hours and dropped 1720 tons of ordnance on targets in South Vietnam. None of its aircraft were seriously damaged, but ground fire hit A-1s during 24 sorties.

During a typical day on *Dixie Station*, VA-176 launched five three-aeroplane missions and one four-aeroplane mission, the last of which recovered at night. Standard 30- and 50-degree dive attacks were used whenever weather and the nature of the target permitted. Racetrack patterns were also flown when ground fire was light or negligible, with 30-to-60 second intervals between attacks to allow FACs to provide target information to the pilot on each run (*text continues on page 65*).

USS *Intrepid* (CVS-11), seen here on 16 December 1965 while working up for its first of three deployments to the Tonkin Gulf, took CVW-10 – the 'Champagne Air Wing' – to Vietnam with an 'all-attack' load-out of two A-4 Skyhawk squadrons (VA-15 and VA-95) and two A-1 Skyraider units (VA-165 and VA-176). CVW-10 was the only air wing to deploy to Vietnam with more than one 'Spad' attack squadron assigned to it (*USN/PH3 F M Horvath*)

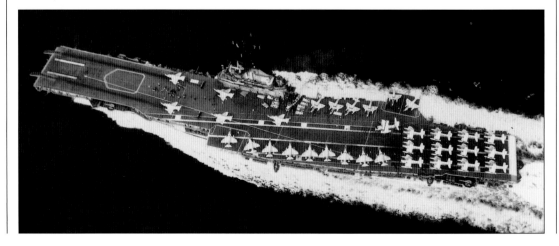

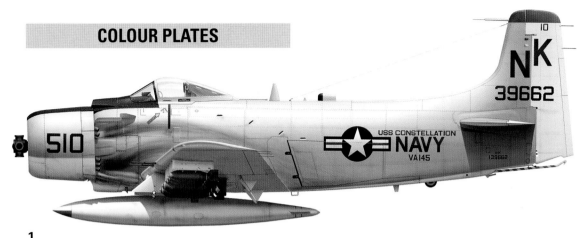

**1**
A-1H BuNo 139662/NK 510 of VA-145, USS *Constellation* (CVA-64), August 1964

**2**
A-1H BuNo 134569/NF 311 of VA-52, USS *Ticonderoga* (CVA-14), August 1964

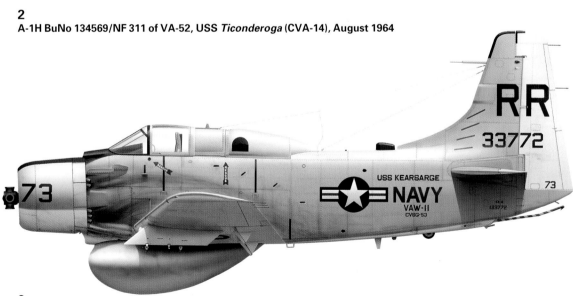

**3**
EA-1E BuNo 133772/RR 73 of VAW-11 Det R, USS *Kearsarge* (CVS-33), September 1964

**4**
A-1H BuNo 139715/NM 605 of VA-196, USS *Bon Homme Richard* (CVA-31), September 1964

**5**
A-1H BuNo 139779/NG 512 of VA-95, USS *Ranger* (CVA-61), March 1965

**6**
A-1H BuNo 139770/NP 565 of VA-215, USS *Hancock* (CVA-19), April 1965

**7**
A-1J BuNo 142035/NL 204 of VA-165, USS *Coral Sea* (CVA-43), July 1965

**8**
EA-1F BuNo 132591/VR 707 of VAW-13 Det 1, 1965

**9**
A-1H BuNo 139768/NE 577 of VA-25, USS *Midway* (CVA-41), September 1965

**10**
A-1J BuNo 142051/AH 582 of VA-152, USS *Oriskany* (CVA-34), August 1965

**11**
A-1H BuNo 139702/NM 601 of VA-196, USS *Bon Homme Richard* (CVA-31), October 1965

**12**
A-1H BuNo 139692/NF 381 of VA-52, USS *Ticonderoga* (CVA-14), March 1966

**13**
A-1H BuNo 139779/NE 574 of VA-25, USS *Coral Sea* (CVA-43), November 1966

**14**
A-1J BuNo 142076/NH 502 of VA-115, USS *Kitty Hawk* (CVA-63), March 1966

**15**
A-1J BuNo 142016/NH501 of VA-115, USS *Kitty Hawk* (CVA-63), December 1965

**16**
A-1J BuNo 142031/NK 504 of VA-145, USS *Ranger* (CVA-61), February 1966

**17**
A-1H BuNo 137512/AH 504 of VA-152, USS *Oriskany* (CVA-34), August 1966

**18**
A-1J BuNo 142059/AK 204 of VA-165, USS *Intrepid* (CVS-11), October 1966

**19**
A-1H BuNo 137543/AK 409 of VA-176, USS *Intrepid* (CVS-11), October 1966

**20**
A-1H BuNo 137586/NP 569 of VA-215, USS *Hancock* (CVA-19), April 1966

**21**
A-1H BuNo 137612/NF 504 of VA-115, USS *Hancock* (CVA-19), June 1967

**22**
A-1H BuNo 134569/NM 300 of VA-52, USS *Ticonderoga* (CVA-14), March 1967

**23**
A-1H BuNo 135324/NP 563 of VA-215, USS *Bonne Homme Richard* (CVA-31), May 1967

**24**
A-1J BuNo 142033/AK 501 of VA-145, USS *Intrepid* (CVS-11), September 1967

**25**
A-1H BuNo 134575/AH 511 of VA-152, USS *Oriskany* (CVA-34), November 1967

**26**
EA-1F BuNo 132591/AK 783 of VAW-33 Det 11,
USS *Intrepid* (CVS-11), November 1967

**27**
A-1H BuNo 135300/NL 405 of VA-25, USS *Coral Sea* (CVA-43), January 1968

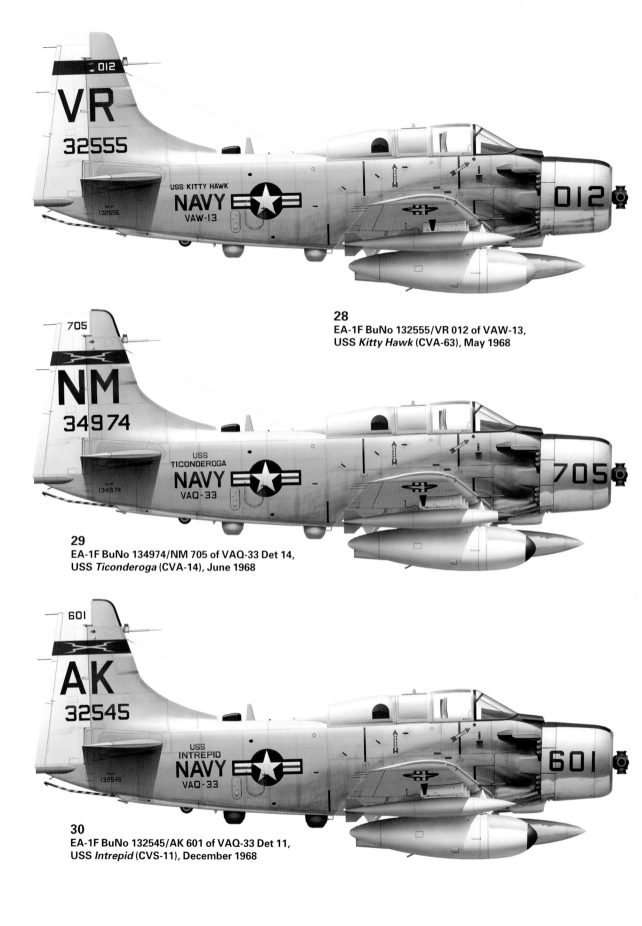

**28**
EA-1F BuNo 132555/VR 012 of VAW-13,
USS *Kitty Hawk* (CVA-63), May 1968

**29**
EA-1F BuNo 134974/NM 705 of VAQ-33 Det 14,
USS *Ticonderoga* (CVA-14), June 1968

**30**
EA-1F BuNo 132545/AK 601 of VAQ-33 Det 11,
USS *Intrepid* (CVS-11), December 1968

**1**

**2**

**3**

**4**

**5**

**6**

**7**

**8**

**9**

**10**

**11**

**12**

**13**

**14**

**15**

**16**

**17**

**18**

**19**

Against more heavily defended targets, the A-1s would roll in at 6000 ft, release ordnance at 4200 ft and pull up by 3000 ft. The common occurrence of a cloud layer at 2500-4000 ft usually necessitated a 30-degree glide from the cloud base. On occasion, Mk 54 depth bombs were used effectively against structures too, whilst 'Daisy cutter' extended fuses proved useful when employed with 2000-lb bombs to clear helicopter landing zones.

Day and night armed reconnaissance accounted for half of the missions flown by VA-165 and VA-176 over North Vietnam. Two-aeroplane sections were used as the primary tactical formation. When four-aeroplane divisions were used, they would split up into two-aeroplane sections and make coordinated attacks from different directions. 'Spads' were limited to lightly defended areas relatively free of SA-2s. However, the mobility of the AAA constantly changed the areas in which they could operate, seriously reducing the effectiveness of what had previously been the best visual reconnaissance aircraft employed over North Vietnam. Pilots had to use 'jinking' and high-g split-S manoeuvres to avoid SAMs. The A-1 also lacked a radar warning receiver system to alert it to the presence of an active SA-2, so 'Spad' pilots had to vigilantly monitor the UHF guard channel for warnings of SAM launches.

'There were so many A-1s on *Intrepid* that planners weren't always sure what to do with us', explained Lt(jg) William T 'Tom' Patton of VA-176. 'Mostly, we were turned loose and told to be careful. In my own case, most of the targets I hit during 40 missions over the north were of my own choosing. We frequently roamed at will, exercising our own judgment, hitting bridges, trucks, barges and the like. We actually blew up two ammo depots and were involved in one "mini" Alpha Strike.'

VA-176 A-1s flew coastal and inland armed reconnaissance in pairs, with not less than 500-700 ft of separation horizontally and vertically. A minimum of 1.5 hours over land was usual during double-cycle missions. A-1s maintained altitudes of 3500-7000 ft, tolerating less effective target acquisition because AAA prohibited lower altitudes.

Most of the remaining missions flown by VA-176 over North Vietnam took the form of RESCAP sorties. CVW-10's A-1s were used in the initial search for downed airmen, as escorts for SAR helicopters

VA-176 A-1H BuNo 135326 is serviced on the deck of CVS-11 in preparation for a mission over Southeast Asia on 20 May 1966. It is armed with Mk 77 mod 1 550-lb napalm fire bombs on the inboard wing pylons. This aircraft was assigned to Lt Charles A Knochel, who was killed in 'Spad' AK 401 BuNo 135239 over North Vietnam on 22 September 1966 – VA-176's only combat loss of the war (*US Navy via Robert F Dorr collection*)

VA-176 A-1H BuNo 137496, assigned to Lt Cdr W C Zimmerman, is refuelled for a launch from CVS-11 in September 1966. The diving bee marking on the empennage became the most famous US Navy Skyraider unit marking of the war (*US Navy/ AN J A Bahrs via R F Dorr collection*)

and HU-16s and for the suppression of AAA and enemy troops. During the deployment, VA-165 and VA-176 flew 108 RESCAP missions, which involved loitering off the coast for up to five hours and being ready at any time to head inland to assist a rescue. The A-1s engaged the enemy during 11 of these missions, resulting in the recovery of six fliers.

Three of *Intrepid's* A-1s were shot down during the deployment, with the first one (A-1H BuNo 137534) being lost on 2 September. The aircraft was being flown by VA-165's XO, Cdr Wiliam S Jett, when it was hit by AAA during a road reconnaissance mission near Vinh Son. Jett managed to reach the Tonkin Gulf and bale out five miles off the coast. He was soon rescued by a US Navy helicopter. Eleven days later, Lt(jg) T J Dwyer's VA-165 A-1H (BuNo 134534) was hit in the port wing by AAA during a strike on an air defence site at Cape Falaise, 25 miles north of Vinh. Like his XO, Dwyer made it to the coast and took to his parachute ten miles out to sea. He too was rescued by a US Navy helicopter.

VA-176 suffered its only combat loss on 22 September when Lt Charles A Knochel drew fire as he went 'feet wet' over Mu Ron Ma after completing an armed reconnaissance mission north of the DMZ. His A-1H (BuNo 135239) was hit in the starboard wing, setting off some of its 20 mm ammunition. Knochel baled out, but he hit the water hard as his parachute swung violently. His wingman saw no movement from the downed aviator when he flew over him, and by the time an HU-16 arrived to attempt a pick-up 12 minutes later, Knochel had slipped beneath the surface of the water and no trace of him was ever found.

On 27 September 1966, Cdr A R Ashworth relieved Martin as CO of VA-176. CVS-11's fourth line period – and its most memorable of the war – began on 1 October. Eight days later, Lt(jg) Patton was on a RESCAP flight led by Lt Cdr Leo Cook, with Lt(jg) Jim Wiley on his wing. Lt Pete Russell led the second section, with Patton on his wing. The weather was fine – excellent visibility and calm seas. The Skyraider pilots knew that they might get some business because they were covering a major three-carrier Alpha strike on targets in the Hanoi area. Three separate groups from each carrier would attack one right after the other. The 'Spads' hugged the coastline southeast of Hanoi, getting as close to 'feet dry' as was safely possible so as to enhance their RESCAP capabilities.

'Looking at the no-man's land between us and the target', said Patton, 'I wondered whether anyone in his right mind would even try to take four A-1s in there. If someone did go down, we'd have to take a direct route to save time, and the direct route would carry us over some deadly flak sites, not to mention SAM emplacements'. Patton and his squadronmates had flown deep into 'Indian Country', as the highly defended region of Hanoi and its environs was sometimes called, numerous times before. But on those occasions they had had the luxury of choosing their entry and exit points, avoiding, wherever possible, enemy gun emplacements.

Plumes of smoke and flame rose from the city's environs as the attacking aircraft dove in and released their bombs. Almost immediately after release, they were winging their way east with all due speed to reach the sanctuary of the sea. At first, Patton thought all the fighters and bombers had escaped enemy guns. However, an F-4B from VF-154 was struck by a 100 mm AAA shell as it rolled in to attack the railway bridge at Phu Ly, forcing the crew to eject 20 miles southwest of Hanoi. Patton

VA-176 A-1H BuNo 135239 had much of its rudder shot away by flak during a mission over North Vietnam. The threat of SA-2 SAMs often drove US aircraft to operate at lower altitudes, where they were vulnerable to radar-guided 37 mm and 57 mm automatic cannons (*US Navy/PH3 J A Bahrs via Robert F Dorr collection*)

examined his navigation charts and the locations of the known SAM and AAA sites, designated by black circles hand-drawn on the chart. There were plenty between the 'Spads' and the F-4 crew. The landscape where the naval aviators had gone down was also characterised by saw-toothed mountains.

'I felt we could get in, but I was worried about the helo's chances. He'd be a sitting duck', Patton recalled. Even so, the decision was made to attempt the rescue. 'I didn't envy Cook having to make the go-ahead decision', Patton continued. 'It was a long shot, but I admired his guts'. Cook and Wiley flew toward land and headed for the shoot-down site, while Patton and Russell, weaving around the slower helicopter, began their ingress. Patton was in the rear, ready to attack any source of ground fire. The flight was made at between 8000-9000 ft – high enough, the A-1 pilots hoped, to escape the known AAA in the enemy's inventory. SAM sites were another matter, for they would have a field day with the 'Spads' and a helicopter at that height.

The latter had enough fuel for a round trip to the ship, plus ten minutes overhead the downed aircrew. Fuel was not a problem for the Skyraiders, as the aircraft's endurance was one of its greatest features.

Once Patton and Russell crossed the coastline the sky around them lit up with flak. Black and white clouds exploded in a startling barrage. 'When I saw that first curtain of AAA, I thought it would be impossible for the helo to get through', explained Patton. 'The pilot must have felt that way, too. Either that, or he became disoriented, for he quickly swung around to the east and began heading back out toward the water'.

Patton directed the helicopter back to the west and the flight continued. 'I rolled in on one of the gun sites', Patton recalled. 'I made several firing passes, scattering 20 mm shells wildly. I thought the runs would keep a few North Vietnamese heads down, but there was no noticeable effect on the volumes of flak. I think the runs boosted the morale of the helo crew, though. Also, I was careful to use only two of my four cannons. I wanted plenty of 20 "mike-mike" on hand for possible use later on. All of a sudden the shooting stopped. It was as if we had passed through a waterfall into the clear. We had made it through unscathed, except for the helo, which took some hits, but none bad enough to cancel the mission'.

Cook then radioed that four MiG-17s had been sighted in the area. Russell promptly transmitted this information to a destroyer offshore, asking for immediate air cover. Unfortunately, the F-4s and F-8s on CAP had run low on fuel, and an in-flight tanker was unavailable. The 'Spad' drivers were on their own. They could muster 240 knots of airspeed at normal rated power, but the MiGs could nearly double that with ease.

Suddenly, Wiley exclaimed, 'I've got three MiGs taking turns on me! Please get some fighter cover in here!' Russell, able to convey some wit even under these pressurised circumstances, keyed his mike and transmitted, 'Right, "Pud", we're on our way with two "Spads" and a helo!'

VA-176 A-1H BuNo 134472, assigned to XO Cdr A R Ashworth, is lifted by crane after it made a gear-up crash landing into the barricade on board CVS-11 on 19 July 1966. The A-1 was flown on this mission by Lt Cdr Charles L Cook, who later became CO of VA-176 in 1968, when the unit retired the last attack 'Spads' in the US Navy. Repaired, BuNo 134472 was supplied to the VNAF, and it is presently on display at the Royal Thai Air Force Museum at Don Muang Airport (*US Navy/PH3 Koennecker via R F Dorr collection*)

Lt(jg) William T 'Tom' Patton stands on the wing of VA-176's A-1H AK 404. Note the MiG silhouette painted with a red lightning bolt through it on the fuselage. Patton was flying in a different aircraft, AK 409 (BuNo 137543), when he downed a MiG-17 on 9 October 1966 (*US Navy via W Mutza collection*)

The survivors were in a mountainous area covered by thick cloud immediately overhead. The four MiGs managed to force Wiley and Cook to separate. One of them then went after Cook, who avoided their line of fire. Wiley was getting the worst of it, however. The remaining MiGs had formed a racetrack pattern and were rolling in on him. His best option was to get down low and make tight turns to elude the jets.

At one point Wiley banked sharply around a mountain to the left. One of the pursuing MiGs broke around the same mountain to the right, then turned steeply to the left. For an instant this placed the MiG in front of Wiley, who gave it a burst from the 'Spad's' cannons. The shells tore off the tip of the MiG's wing and a vapour trail spurted from it. No one saw the MiG crash, but Wiley was later credited with a 'probable kill.'

Patton said, 'Pete and I arrived right after that with the helo. We were strung out, spotted two of the MiGs, and manoeuvred for a head-on pass'. Russell had his cannons armed, and he aimed at the belly of the lead MiG. It sped directly toward him, and he fired. The MiG passed so close that Russell's A-1 shook from the wake created by the jet's exhaust. Although the MiG was not seen again, Russell was also credited with a probable kill.

Meanwhile, Patton was still at 9000 ft. 'I shoved the throttle forward to full power, then pushed over. A MiG darting along above the trees was heading in my direction, but its pilot didn't see me. I counted for four seconds until I figured he was in range, then rolled my A-1 into a split-S. I dove straight down, gathering speed to 300+ knots and completed the split at the MiG's "four o'clock", pulling Gs to recover from the dive'.

The dive seemed to be too steep, but Patton fired anyway. Then the MiG pilot realised the A-1 was on him, and he pulled up hard towards it.

'Thinking that I would overshoot him, he executed a reverse turn', Patton continued. 'This was a fatal mistake on his part. He was climbing, losing speed, while I still had plenty. Maybe his reversal would have worked against another MiG-17, but in this case it was premature on his part because I ended up at his "six o'clock". I'd been tight as a clenched fist till this point, but now I felt myself relax, knowing the advantage I had.'

'I waited patiently until the MiG filled my gunsight reticle. This was, of course, the most exciting moment in my life. I'll never forget it. The most obvious first impression I had when up close to the enemy fighter was the "coke bottle" shape of the fuselage. The only marking I remember was the red star midway along the fuselage. Both the MiG and I were climbing, me in close trail on him. I fired the cannons. My wings trembled, and the 20 "mike-mike" sounded a reassuring, deep staccato as they streamed into the tailpipe of the MiG. I was so close I could see metal fragments flying from the tail, which was literally disintegrating.

'I started firing at 500 ft and closed to 100 ft. Both the MiG and I were pointed up at a 75-degree angle when my guns quit. I later learned that two were empty and the other pair had jammed. The MiG

This was the A-1H (BuNo 137543) that Lt(jg) W Thomas 'Tom' Patton was flying when he shot down his MiG-17 on 9 October 1966. It is seen here parked on the apron at NAS Quonset Point, Rhode Island, in 1968, awaiting overhaul, repainting and transfer to the USAF for combat duty in Southeast Asia This aircraft was shot down near Muong Soui, in Laos, on 2 July 1969, killing its pilot, Capt John L Flinn (*Roger Besecker via Wayne Mutza collection*)

Lt(jg) W Thomas 'Tom' Patton (left) and Lt Peter F Russell describe their MiG-killing mission of 9 October 1966, standing in front of A-1H BuNo 135326 AK 412 which the latter pilot was flying at the time. Russell went on to fly OV-10A Bronco aircraft with Light Attack Squadron Four in South Vietnam, and was killed by small-arms fire on 23 May 1969 (*US Navy via Robert F Dorr collection*)

A-1H BuNo 135272 *SHUSH BOOMER* of VA-165 was assigned to Lt Jeb Stuart. It is seen here flying over the Tonkin Gulf in 1966. A veteran of two Vietnam tours with the A-1, VA-165 was nicknamed the 'Boomers'. The unit subsequently completed no fewer than five combat tours with the A-6 Intruder between November 1967 and October 1973 (*Tom Hansen via Wayne Mutza collection*)

still hadn't exploded, so I fired three Zunis one right after the other'.

The Zunis had straight, true trajectories. They burst from their chambers in the four-place pods beneath each wing but zoomed by the MiG, narrowly missing it.

'The MiG then flipped over and plummeted toward a mass of clouds below. I bent my aircraft around and followed him. Just before the MiG disappeared into the white mass, I fired the last rocket, which must have missed also. Enveloped by cloud, I switched my visual scan to the gauges in order to right myself. I wasn't keen to smash into one of the surrounding mountains. I popped clear at 500 ft and was bottoming out from the dive when, off to my left, I saw the pilot eject from the MiG.'

The helicopter crew saw some of the action from their position above the clouds, but not the ejection or the crash. Leo Cook and the others were several miles away, and did not see what went on either, but in short order they flew over the crash site. Patton received official credit for the kill based on the helicopter crew's observations and Cook's authentication of the crash site. It was later learned that four MiGs had launched but only three had returned to base, one with a seriously damaged wingtip.

'I think the 20 "mike-mike" disabled the engine', noted Patton. 'Maybe the MiG pilot made that last plunge through the clouds to reach a lower altitude at which to eject. Perhaps he felt that punching out earlier would have made him a helpless target floating down in his 'chute.'

Sadly, the F-4 crew that the flight had been trying to rescue was captured soon after reaching the ground. Subsequently, Patton was awarded the Silver Star, while Cook, Wiley and Russell received DFCs. Russell completed the CVS-11 deployment, volunteered for more combat duty, this time in OV-10s with Light Attack Squadron Four, and was killed in his aircraft by a single bullet over South Vietnam on 23 May 1969.

The damage inflicted on the communist war effort by VA-176, for example, is reflected in the unit's statistics – 14 bridges, 84 barges, 15 trucks, 17 rail cars and three AAA sites destroyed, with other targets in these categories damaged. The 'Thunderbolts' accomplished these feats in 1606 combat sorties with 2566 tons of ordnance. *Intrepid* and CVW-10 arrived home on 21 November. The following month, Cdr Jett relieved Parode as CO of VA-165. The unit then moved to NAS Whidbey Island, Washington, for transition to the A-6A, and it would return to the war with its new jet in November 1967.

# THE 'FIST' RETURNS

On 13 April 1966, Cdr William J Stoddard relieved Cdr Harry E Ettinger as CO of VA-25, which was soon assigned (along with the rest of CVW-2) to *Midway's* sister ship, *Coral Sea*, for its second war cruise. The unit went straight into action on 13 September, just 24 hours after arriving in-theatre, when Lt Cdr Rosario M 'Zip' Rausa – on his first flight of the war – and Lt Charlie W Hartman participated in the successful extraction of an F-105 pilot downed over Laos.

The next day, however, saw the loss of Cdr Stoddard during an armed reconnaissance mission. Three SA-2s were fired at his A-1H (BuNo 139756) shortly after he had led his section on a strike against a storage facility near Vinh. Stoddard and his wingman, Lt Cdr Ralph Smith, were descending from 5000 ft down to 1000 ft just off the coast when the first two missiles exploded nearby. The CO's warning of SAMs in the air enabled his wingman to avoid the SA-2s, but the third destroyed Stoddard's A-1, killing him instantly. VA-25's XO, Cdr James D Burden, assumed command of the unit without ceremony later that same day.

By this time, armed reconnaissance and RESCAP were the primary missions of A-1 units in the Tonkin Gulf, with dedicated strikes having been consigned to the past due to the SAM threat. Highways, bridges, supply depots, barges, junks and truck convoys were the main targets. VA-25 operated mostly over and offshore of central North Vietnam. Frequently, night road reconnaissance was conducted in coordination with sophisticated US Army OV-1 Mohawk observation aircraft.

On 12 October, Lt R Deane Wood's A-1H (BuNo 135323) was hit by AAA near Lang Long during a reconnaissance mission along Route 15. The pilot headed for the coast, but his starboard wing was soon ablaze, and he baled out over enemy territory. Landing on a hillside, Wood hid beneath a thick jungle canopy and waited to be rescued. A-1s assisted in the SAR effort, but ground fire drove away a Sea King SAR helicopter sent to pick him up. On 16 October, a team of US Special Forces and Nung commandos from Laos was inserted by two Sea Kings from *Intrepid*, and they searched the area for several hours, killing four enemy soldiers. With North Vietnamese troops closing in on Wood's position, the commandos were retrieved by two Sea Kings, but one SH-3 was hit by ground fire, wounding two crewmen and two commandos. The stricken helicopter ditched near the destroyer USS *Henley* (DD-762), which rescued the crew and commandos.

During the last of these failed rescue attempts, VA-25's Lt(jg) Al Nichols escorted a helicopter through an overcast and made repeated strafing and rocket-firing runs with only 700 ft between the

VA-25 A-1H Skyraiders share the deck of *Coral Sea* with other CVW-2 aircraft in 1966 during the squadron's second Vietnam deployment. Aircraft NE 575 (foreground) is loaded with Mk 81 250-lb low-drag bombs fitted with Snakeye fins. The latter allowed the aircraft to release the bombs at lower speeds and altitudes without endangering the aircraft. BuNo 127517 was ultimately supplied to the VNAF (*National Museum of Naval Aviation via Wayne Mutza collection*)

cloud layer and the ground. Woods ordered the SAR helicopter away from his position, however, because of the proximity of enemy troops. He was captured a short while later and eventually released on 4 March 1973.

On 6 November, Lt Cdr Smith and Ens Larry Gardiner participated in the rescue of an F-105 pilot downed well inside enemy territory. Five days later, Lt Jim Lynne and Gardiner located a VA-22 A-4C pilot who had ejected near the coast after colliding with his wingman. They covered the downed aviator until he was rescued by a US Navy helicopter.

18 November saw Lt Cdr J D Ehret and Lt(jg) Bruce G Marcus targeted by three SA-2s that were fired at them whilst they were flying five miles inland west of Hon Me Island. Two of the SAMs detonated near Marcus' 'Spad', but he was able to survive the attack through the employment of well-executed tactics. This incident, combined with the recent loss of A-1s from other units to SAMs, led to the restriction of all US Navy Skyraiders to RESCAP, coastal reconnaissance, divert recoveries in Laos and controlled bombing in the vicinity of the DMZ. A-1s were also prohibited from flying over North Vietnam, except during SAR missions.

'Spads' also routinely carried out naval gunfire spotting, with pilots acting as the aerial 'eyes' for destroyers on the Operation *Sea Dragon* gun line just north of the DMZ, as well as for vessels firing at coastal shipping.

1967 had barely begun when, on 5 January, two VA-25 A-1s were involved in the attempted rescue of VA-192 A-4E pilot Lt Cdr Richard A Stratton. Ejecting over the Kidney River, near Thanh Hoa, he had been captured almost immediately. Disappointment also struck on 13 January when a VA-23 A-4E pilot ejected near Hon Me Island. Parachuting into the water offshore, the naval aviator was blown ashore and captured. Three VA-25 A-1s took hits from ground fire during the rescue attempt.

Later that same month, in a departure from routine, four 'Spads' led by Gardiner were directed against a large force of troops four battalions strong in southern Laos. Each A-1 made four runs, but the results were undetermined. VA-25 returned to Lemoore on 23 February 1967 and immediately began preparing for its third, and last, war cruise with the Skyraider, which would commence in just five months time.

## 'WILD ACES HIGH'

VA-152, with Cdr Gordon H Smith as CO, deployed with CVW-16 on *Oriskany* for its second Vietnam cruise on 26 May 1966. Arriving on *Dixie Station* on 30 June, the unit warmed up with 128 sorties in just eight days against VC troops and bases, prior to CVA-34 being transferred to *Yankee Station*. One of VA-152's first duties 'up north' was to cover the rescue of VF-162 F-8E pilot Lt(jg) Richard F Adams (his second ejection over Vietnam) on 12 July northeast of Haiphong. Four 'Wild Aces" A-1s were involved in the SAR mission, which penetrated deeper into North Vietnam than any preceding rescue attempt. VA-152 also assisted in the rescue of two USAF pilots near Dong Hoi on 27 July.

The 'O Boat's' second line period got off to a sad start on 7 August when Lt Charles W Fryer's A-1H (BuNo 139701) was hit in its port wing by small arms fire while attacking a train near Qui Vinh. Fryer attempted to ditch in the Tonkin Gulf off Cape Bouton, but did not survive. The mood of the squadron was brightened a few days later by two successful SAR missions. Two VF-111 F-8E pilots were rescued from coastal waters on 11 and 13 August with assistance from VA-152. Also on 13 August, Smith and Lt(jg) J M Watson destroyed a PT boat near Hon Gay.

VA-152 enjoyed a spectacular success on 18 August during a road reconnaissance mission near Cape Bang when Lt Cdr Eric Schade and Lt A J Garvey noticed tracks leading into a wooded area. On a hunch, Schade fired several Zunis into the woods, setting off several secondary explosions. Every subsequent rocket and strafing run yielded more explosions. Three more pairs of VA-152 A-1s joined the strike in succession,

all producing more secondary explosions. The strike resulted in the destruction of an estimated 22 trucks and 300-800 barrels of fuel. The burned-out clearing became known as 'Eric's Truck Park'.

The successful VA-152 SAR of a USAF pilot near Ha Cong on 20 August was followed by the loss of two 'Spads'. Five days later, Lt(jg) James A Beene escaped from his A-1H (BuNo 135236) after it ditched in front of *Oriskany* following the failure of a catapult holdback fitting. Then on the 28th, Cdr Smith's A-1H (BuNo 135231) was hit by AAA 25 miles south of Thanh Hoa. Heading out over the Tonkin Gulf with the fuselage of his aircraft burning fiercely, Smith kicked himself vertically out of the cockpit, but struck the tail as he fell away from the Skyraider. Fortunately, his parachute deployed before he hit the water, and Smith was rescued by a US Navy helicopter launched from a nearby destroyer.

On 31 August two A-1s covered the rescue of a VFP-63 RF-8G pilot from Haiphong harbour. A POL (petroleum, oil, lubricant) storage area near Lang Ha was hit by the unit on 7 September, and the next day VA-152 destroyed 17 trucks. Two bridges were dropped on 24 September.

*Oriskany's* last line period on *Yankee Station* for the deployment would end with disaster, both for the ship and CVW-16. On 5 October, Lt(jg) Beene, who survived his catapult-related ditching on 25 August, was lost with his A-1H (BuNo 137610) in a thunderstorm 15 miles south of Hon Mat island – only an oil slick was later found on the surface of the water.

Three days later, Lt John A Feldhaus' A-1H (BuNo 137629) was hit by AAA during a road reconnaissance mission near Lang Quang. His wingman, Lt(jg) Quenzel, was also hit, which meant that he was unable to loiter to assist Feldhaus, who died in the resulting crash.

Ammunition dumps, POL storage and trucks were hit hard by the unit in succeeding days, but on 14 October Ens Darwin J Thomas was killed when his A-1H (BuNo

A catapult officer touches the flightdeck to signal the launch go-ahead for a VA-152 Skyraider from *Oriskany* in 1966. The aircraft is being despatched on a naval gunfire-spotting mission in support of *Sea Dragon* off North Vietnam. A UH-2 helicopter on a plane-guard mission hovers in the background (*US Navy/Lt J M Watson III via Wayne Mutza collection*)

VA-52 was one of only three US Navy Skyraider squadrons involved in the Vietnam War known to have flown a 'CAG' bird, as denoted by the modex NM 300. The squadron's tradition of painting its bomb racks (blue in colour) can be seen in this 1967 photograph of A-1H BuNo 134569, the 'Knightrider's' 'CAG bird', at Da Nang, loaded with 12 260-lb anti-personnel fragmentation bombs. Note the unusual white section of the engine cowling. This aircraft was also passed on to the VNAF (*Tom Hansen via Wayne Mutza collection*)

Cdr George Carlton (left), commanding officer of VA-215 'Barn Owls', with Cdr Jack Monger, commander of CVW-21, in 1967 during the unit's third Vietnam deployment. Carlton is wearing a Nomex fire-retardant flight suit, a new Life Preserver Assembly and a G-suit. Monger is wearing a 'Mae West' life preserver. Note the gun belt around his waist (*US Navy via George Carlton*)

139731) crashed while making a rocket run during a night road reconnaissance mission near Nai Chuot Bach.

VA-152's losses were not yet over, for on 26 October, *Oriskany* suffered a devastating fire. Six A-1s and seven A-4s were on the flightdeck being readied for a night strike that evening when bad weather postponed the launch. These aircraft were fully armed when the postponement order was issued, so all ordnance had to be downloaded and stored until it was required again. During the course of this operation, a Mk 24 Model 3 magnesium parachute flare was mishandled and ignited in the forward hangar deck area. The fire that erupted then detonated ordnance elsewhere in the hangar deck that was being prepared for an air strike.

The resulting conflagration took more than five hours to put out, by which point 36 officers (including 24 naval aviators) and eight enlisted men had perished. Among the dead were VA-152's XO, Cdr John J Nussbaumer, and AZAN David A Liste. *Oriskany* left the line and returned to Alameda on 16 November, whereupon it entered Hunter Point shipyard in San Francisco for repairs to be effected.

The vessel's 1966 cruise was one of the more costly carrier deployments of the war in terms of aircraft and pilots lost. Some 28 aircraft were destroyed (16 by enemy action and 12 in mishaps) and 34 naval aviators killed or captured during the course of the deployment.

1967 would see the last deployments in 'Spads' for the US Navy's six remaining A-1 attack units. Amongst the latter was VA-52 (with Cdr Robert Worchesek as CO), which joined CVW-19 again on board CVA-14 when the vessel departed Alameda on 15 October 1966. The squadron was fortunate in that 14 of its 21 pilots were combat veterans. During four line periods, the 'Knightriders' flew mostly RESCAP and coastal recconnaissance patrols, as well as a few *Steel Tiger* missions. VA-52 pilots also acted as gunfire spotters for surface ships involved in *Sea Dragon*.

Lt W H Natter's A-1H (BuNo 135341) was hit by machine gun fire on 27 November while he was attacking coastal barges 15 miles north of Thanh Hoa. He was rescued by a US Navy helicopter after ditching his burning aircraft 40 miles out into the Tonkin Gulf. On 18 January 1967, Lt(jg) Marlow E Madsen (in A-1H BuNo 139748), who was returning to CVA-14 after a combat mission, was unable to slow his speed for a safe arrestment. Waved off, he stalled, crashed into the sea and was killed.

The 'Knightriders' returned home on 29 May and immediately prepared for their move to NAS Whidbey Island and transition to the A-6A Intruder. Vietnam would see them again in September 1968.

VA-215 also found itself in-theatre in early 1967 conducting its last A-1 deployment. Led by Cdr George Carlton, the unit left Alameda with the rest of CVW-21 on 26 January 1967, but this time embarked in *Bon Homme Richard*. Carlton recounted one of his more memorable missions;

'Our first night attempt to rescue a downed pilot in enemy territory occurred on 22 May 1967. A USAF F-4 had crashed some 30 miles north of Hon Gay, and the chain-of-command – Cdr Jack Monger (CAG-21), Capt C K Ruiz (CO of the *Bonne Homme Richard*) and Rear Adm Vincent P de Poix (Commander, Carrier Group 7) – wanted to talk to me in the flag ops centre. They had alerted the northern SAR ship to have a helo in readiness. We all studied the charts, complete with AAA and SAM plots, and I recommended a go. Someone was concerned that the location

A-1H BuNo 135300 flies wing on an HU-16 in 1966. This aircraft was one of the four VA-25 Skyraiders that prevailed over a VPAF MiG-17 in June 1965. The aircraft was transferred to VA-52, shown here, and later returned to VA-25, with whom it flew the last US Navy A-1 attack mission of the war. BuNo 135300 is preserved in the National Museum of Naval Aviation at NAS Pensacola, Florida (*Tom Hansen via Wayne Mutza collection*)

was too close to MiG bases at Kep, but it was agreed that VPAF fighters were not known to fly at night.

'Monger asked, "What will you need?" Being used to the SAR mission, I quickly advised him that we would required four A-1s, four F-8s, one A-3 tanker and the "Willie Fudd" (E-1B Tracer). "What load?" Monger enquired."We'll need full fuel, full ammo (800 rounds of 20 mm), two rocket pods (19-shot 2.75-in FFARs) and two flares on each bird". This was a light load for the Skyraider, allowing us to make good speed to the objective area.

'We would to stagger the launches, with the E-1 going first, followed by the A-1s, A-3 and the F-8s – all separated by 15 to 20 minutes, thereby allowing us all to arrive on station at the same time with maximum fuel.

'We decided to start at 2100 hrs, which would put us all on station by 2215 hrs. The helo was ready to go, and I planned to pick it up as we passed the northern SAR destroyer, well up into the Tonkin Gulf. As all of this was starting, I had just returned from an uneventful RESCAP – no SAR mission had developed, but we did shoot up some "Wiblicks". As we were leaving the flag briefing room, CAG asked me, "Who's leading this one?" He knew the answer. Squadron COs fly more hours, and invariably lead first-of-a-kind missions. This would not be an exception.

'I remembered standing in the VA-215 ready room on *Hancock* in early 1965 when Bob Hessom was the "Barn Owl" CO. At the time I was on CTF-77's staff, and was down there to be around the "Spad" drivers and see how things were going. Little did I know that I would join the unit a year later as XO. As Bob was suiting up for a hop, the ops officer, working on the next day's schedule, suggested that the skipper might want to take the day off, for he was well ahead on flight hours. Bob stared him down, offering that this was his war, his squadron and his flight schedule! I fully supported that "Barn Owl" tradition. This would not be an exception.

'The launch, join-up and flight north went well. As we approached the SAR ship, I sent my Nos 3 and 4 off to escort the helo to a point ten miles southeast of Cam Pha to await my orders. With the E-1, F-8s and A-3 in position south and east of Cam Pha, we were all set to have a go at it.

'As I approached the off-shore islands northeast of Cam Pha, having determined that our path of least resistance would be along an easterly route about ten miles north of here, I detached my wingman to provide high cover for the helo on the way in. Thinking that a single "Spad" throttled back to 160 knots would cause less of a stir, I turned off the external lights and proceeded in at an altitude of about 2000 ft, throttling back and leaning the carburettor mixture so as to reduce the exhaust flames as much as possible. In rich mixture, the R-3350 engine put out huge, bright red exhaust trails along both sides of the fuselage. On the other hand, in lean mixture the exhaust was a soft, light blue colour. It was about as stealthy as one could get in a Skyraider.

'"So far so good", I was thinking, as I could see some lights from Hon Gay at my "nine-thirty". Thinking that I must be within five miles of our estimated datum, I tried the first contact. "Starlight Four", this is "Barn Owl One", over.'

'Magically, he came back with, "Barn Owl", you're loud and clear.'

'"Show me a light", I responded. Starting a turn to set up an orbit, out of the blackness below a dim light appeared. '"Kill it", I radioed. The light went out. "Barn Owl Three", bring 'em in. The datum's good.' "Roger, out", was the response.

'I gently climbed to the east, thinking that lady luck was with us on this one. At 130 knots, it would take the helo 20 minutes to make the transit. The F-8s moved overland as high cover, the A-3 tanker was just offshore, ready to refuel them and the E-1, 50 miles south, had a radar view of the whole scene. During the helo transit, I climbed up to 6000 ft and then eased back into position to be ready with guns and rockets as needed.

'I could see the helicopter approaching the datum, showing a vertical white light for identification and coordination purposes. He was in charge for the pick-up. After an exchange with the downed airman, who was assured by the helo crew that he had a good shot at being rescued, the pilot started his approach to a hover. All was looking okay from my perch at 6000 ft. Suddenly, the blackness erupted as I could see muzzle flashes from positions a half-mile or so west of the scene. Immediately thereafter, the helo pilot reported, "We've been hit. My co-pilot's wounded".

'As I was rolling in on the flashes, I radioed, "Abort! Abort! 'Barn Owls' get out too", as I didn't want to take out one of my own birds.

'After flipping on the master arming switch (the four 20 mm cannons were already set to fire) and turning the external lights to bright and flashing, I steadied in the run and fired my weapons in bursts – I feared that they would overheat and jam if fired continuously – at the muzzle flashes now coming in my direction. The tracers were going right into the flashes as I pressed home the attack. The AAA diminished, and I became concerned about when to pull up, not knowing how high the terrain was. Thinking that I was well below normal weapons release altitude, I squeezed off one more burst and pulled the stick back as hard as I dared, at the same time pushing throttle, prop and mixture controls full forward. Thankfully, the A-1 climbed like the proverbial homesick angel.

'A check with the helo revealed that he would be feet wet in 15 minutes, and that the co-pilot was stable. I throttled back and headed downhill west of Cam Pha. Nearing the coast at 500 ft and 300 knots, AAA flashes began blinking brightly off my left wing. "My God", I thought, "They're firing at me!" Realising that my external lights were still on bright and flashing, I cut them and stood the A-1 on its right wingtip, pulling the nose through 45 degrees. Levelling the wings and seeing the coastline ahead, I continued downhill, crossing the beach at no more than 50 ft.

'The emotions one feels upon going feet wet after hanging it out a bit over a hostile beach are unparalleled. In the process, I radioed blindly (not wanting a response) "Keep moving. We'll be back". I didn't know when,

VA-215 A-1H BuNo 135324 is towed at Da Nang AB in 1967. VA-215 teamed with CVW-21 for three Vietnam deployments. The third, during which this photograph was taken, saw the unit embarked in *Bonne Homme Richard* (*Tom Hansen via Wayne Mutza collection*)

but I wanted "Starlight Four" to evade as best he could. He certainly knew where the hostile fire was coming from, and should move off in the opposite direction – his best chance to avoid being captured.

'I picked up the other three "Barn Owls" over the north SAR ship just as the helo landed. We then headed back to CVA-31 for our night landings – a piece of cake compared to recent events. With an angled deck, mirror-aided glide path and the drop line for line-up reference, we had come a long way from the old days of straight decks and "Paddles".

'After debriefing with VA-215's air intelligence officer, I headed for Air Ops, where they had set up a radio link with my counterpart, Cdr Hank Bailey, CO of VA-115, in CVA-19. As "Bonnie Dick" would be off-line for replenishment the next day, the SAR job would pass to *Hancock*.

'Hank and I had been squadronmates in our first unit, VA-15, flying AD-4s under the able leadership of John Lacouture and then Roy Isaman – two of the best "sticks" in the business. As nuggets and Flying Midshipmen, it was our good fortune to start out with those two guys. Over the years, I had often asked myself when in tight situations (both flying and administrative), "What would John and Roy do?" For better or worse, your first skippers are always with you. Hank and I discussed the SAR scene, and the best routes in and out. I wished him luck and headed for the showers. It was now well passed midnight – all in a day's work.'

One of the F-4 crewmen was rescued successfully the next day, but the second was captured.

VA-215 lost two pilots during this final A-1 deployment. Lt Paul C Charvet was killed on 21 March 1967 when his A-1H (BuNo 137516) crashed in poor weather near Hon Me Island during a *Sea Dragon* patrol. The cause of his demise was never determined. Ens Richard C Graves perished on 25 May – probably a victim of shore-based AAA – when his A-1H (BuNo 135366) plunged into the sea during a rocket attack on WBLCs 15 miles north of Vinh. Upon returning to Alameda on 25 August 1967, VA-215 was disestablished. A new VA-215, carrying on the traditions of the 'Barn Owls', would take to the skies in A-7B Corsair IIs in March 1968 and see combat again in Vietnam in January 1969.

## "ARABS" IN THE WATER

VA-115 joined CVW-5 from CVW-11 in July 1966, at which point Cdr H G 'Hank' Bailey became CO of the 'Arabs'. The unit returned to the Tonkin Gulf in late January 1967 on board *Hancock*, and found itself engaged mostly in gunfire spotting and reactive strikes for the cruisers and destroyers involved in *Sea Dragon*. During one month alone, the 'Arabs' destroyed 350 barges, 85 trucks, 50 buildings and 16 bridges. VA-115 also assisted in the rescue of ten downed airmen during the deployment.

VA-115 incurred its first loss of the cruise on 14 February 1967, when Lt Robert C Marvin suffered engine failure (in A-1H BuNo 139805) soon after launching with his wingman on a RESCAP mission. He reported that he was losing oil pressure, and both A-1s turned around and headed back to CVA-19. The wingman lost sight of Marvin's aircraft, however, and it was presumed that he ditched 25 miles east of Mu Ron Ma. The subsequent search for Marvin (who had completed 111 missions during VA-115's previous combat cruise aboard *Kitty Hawk* in 1965-66) failed to turn up any sign of either him or his aircraft.

On 17 March, VA-115 suffered the worst single-day losses of any US Navy Skyraider squadron during the Vietnam War. During an armed reconnaissance flight over the southern provinces of North Vietnam, two A-1Hs flown by Lt Cdr A H 'Arnie' Henderson (BuNo 135297) and Lt R B Moore (BuNo 139768) were hit by automatic weapons fire as they pulled up from an attack on a barge in the mouth of the Sou Giang River. Henderson ditched ten miles offshore while Moore abandoned his aircraft near a freighter – both men were rescued. Several hours later, two more A-1Hs were lost in a mid-air collision at night over the Gulf of Tonkin during a SAR mission. Lt(jg) Gene W Goeden (in BuNo 135225) was killed, but Cdr Bailey (in BuNo 134625) was rescued.

Capt (then Lt Cdr) Cliff Johns recalled this black day for VA-115;

'It all began after I had just finished a 4.7-hour armed recce flight over North Vietnam that could be described as routine, if any combat sortie is ever routine. Word came in that two of our squadron aircraft had been shot down. That was unusual enough, two together, apparently shot down in a flak trap diving through a thin overcast after some derelict boats. Bad luck on our part, but good tactics on the part of the enemy.

'Then, soon after dusk, and under the lowering overcast, the skipper got the tail section of his Skyraider cut off by his wingman's prop when he suddenly instigated a sharp turn so as to avoid a helo that was trying to manoeuvre for the rescue pick-up of "Arnie" Henderson. Confusion!

'Our XO had just reported aboard, and was still making maps and getting oriented. I was next in terms of seniority, being the operations officer. So after dark, tired already, and apprehensive about my roommate and friends out there somewhere in the water, I launched, leading three others to try and find, defend and save our squadronmates.

'When we arrived on the scene, the overcast was down to 500 ft – it was solid and it was really dark. Any naval aviator who has been out there alone over water on a dark night knows what I am talking about. Others will just have to imagine walking into a strange house at night with no lights on and finding a coat closet to bang around in. That's what we call actual instrument conditions – no visual reference. Worst still, there was occasional lightning, mortar rounds and no radar in our ageing "Spads".

'I found the skipper and "Arnie" Henderson by homing on their UHF transmissions, but it was tough because they kept cutting each other out since they couldn't hear the other guy transmit. When this happened, my homing needle ("Bird Dog") spun crazily. I kept all of my wingmen on top of the overcast to avoid yet another mishap. They were ordered to drop flares on my signal by homing in on our transmissions – a crude, but effective, method.

'The problem was that parachute-retarded flares swinging back and forth under that overcast, mixed with lightning and the occasional mortar round, promoted continuous and rather violent vertigo – the complete

Two VA-115 A-1Hs fly wing on a USAF HU-16B Albatross amphibian, from which this photograph was taken, in 1967 during the 'Arabs'' second Vietnam deployment, this time with CVW-5 on board *Hancock*. The aircraft are each armed with two pods of four 5-in Zuni rockets and four 19-shot pods of 2.75-in rockets – a typical load for a RESCAP. The A-1 furthest from the camera (BuNo 134526) was subsequently transferred to the VNAF (*Tom Hansen via Wayne Mutza collection*)

loss of one's natural balance and reference mechanisms, and not conducive to safe instrument flying conditions. I almost flew into the water on several occasions as I banked hard over the CO or "Arnie", trying to drop a flare on top or guide the second helo in for a rescue pick-up.

'The skipper was in shock by this time, with severe bruises to the head and ears and a compound fracture of the arm. His radio discipline broke down over the course of the five-and-a-half hours it took us to get them out, but when I saw him back on CVA-19 I could see why. His ears looked exactly like mature Idaho potatoes, his face was swollen and badly distorted and the bone in his forearm was exposed through the skin. He was also half-a-mile off the coast of Vinh, drifting slowly ashore. "Arnie" was healthier, but closer in, and had been in the water three hours longer.

'I never did find out who the second helo driver was. He was from another ship, but I hope he got the Silver Star, because he deserved it. I was at the end of my rope when he arrived – out of ideas and stamina at the same time. Nevertheless, he followed me in, quietly and professionally, went into a hover, ignored all of the distractions and picked up "Arnie" on the first pass. I never could see the rafts they were in, but at 180 knots and 200 ft at night under an overcast, it was just too much to expect. When the helo pilot got my mark on top of the skipper and announced his pick-up minutes later, I almost cried in relief. My fuel state was 600 lbs, which even in the old "Spad" was well below minimums, with no possible divert and no good idea where the carrier may have gone.

'It was a great, blessed relief just to be able to put the power on and climb out of that hell hole through the clouds and to finally see the moon. What a terrific sight! I will never forget that feeling, and how grateful I was that my training included many hours "under the bag" in instrument school in Link trainers and simulators, and later as a squadron pilot. Not only did that training save my life, but I guess I'm the only one who can say that what we did really saved the skipper's and "Arnie's" too.

'We found out later that the skipper's wingman had not survived the mid-air collision, and that "Arnie's" wingman had stayed airborne for another two hours after being hit and then ditched next to a freighter.

'After I landed (with 200 lbs of fuel remaining), I downed a medicinal brandy with "Arnie" and visited the CO in the sick bay. I privately offered my sincere prayer of thanks, because all things considered, I wasn't so sure that I wasn't the luckiest one of all – 5.5 hours at night under that overcast off Vinh ended the longest day of my life in the most successful way possible. We got all but one back aboard from a bizarre situation that involved ten of our pilots, any one of whom could have "bought the farm" that day.'

VA-115 returned to Lemoore on 22 July 1967 and stood down to a cadre status. The unit would resume operational service in January 1970 with A-6As, and return to Vietnam in April 1971.

This VA-115 A-1H, seen in the summer of 1967, was assigned to Lt Cdr Jack Jones. It bears one of the more unusual personalised markings seen on a US Navy Skyraider – black-paint footprints of a three-toed person! This aircraft carries seven-shot 2.75-in rockets pods on the outboard wing stations rather than the more common 19-shot pods. Handed over to the USAF following its retirement by VA-115, BuNo 137612 was shot down over South Vietnam on 5 May 1968 and its pilot, Capt Lyn D Oberdier, killed (*Tom Hansen via Wayne Mutza collection*)

# INTREPID 'SWORDSMEN'

Having completed two previous war cruises with CVW-14, VA-145 undertook its third, and final, Vietnam tour with CVW-10, embarked in *Intrepid*. Led by Cdr Donald E Sparks, the unit replaced VA-165 and VA-176 within the air wing in late 1966.

Pre-deployment training took a toll on the unit, for on 17 November 1966 Lt Cdr Tinley L Olton was killed when, during a low-level pass against a small craft, his 'Spad' (BuNo 139654) hit the boat's mast and crashed into the sea off California. Then on 23 January 1967, Lt Cdr A D Windsor suffered engine failure in his A-1H (BuNo 134563) at Fallon, Nevada, forcing him to make a gear-up landing that wrote his aircraft off.

CVS-11 deployed on 11 May 1967 and arrived on *Yankee Station* on 19 June. Because of a shortage of 'Spads', VA-145 had only eight A-1s assigned, and it used these to perform its primary mission – RESCAP. The unit also conducted armed reconnaissance and naval gunfire spotting as secondary missions. At times during the deployment, VA-145 was the only A-1 unit on *Yankee Station*.

The 'Swordsmen' typically flew with centreline 300-gallon fuel tanks, allowing them to perform 4.5-hour cycles. For RESCAP, the 'Spads' were usually armed with full 20 mm ammunition, up to four rocket pods and two Mk 6 smoke lights. For armed reconnaissance and naval gunfire spotting, the 'Swordsmen' often added two Mk 81 250-lb bombs to this load.

VA-145 flew its first SAR mission of the deployment on 28 June to cover a VF-143 F-4B crew downed in North Vietnam. Unfortunately, Cdr (later Vice Adm) William P Lawrence and Lt(jg) James Bailey were captured, despite the SAR efforts. The next SAR mission, on 2 July, had a happier outcome. Lt Cdr R Alvarez and Lt(jg) W S 'Walt' Bumgarner escorted a UH-2 to the scene of a downed USAF F-105 pilot 30 miles inland. The two 'Spads' silenced AAA in the area and the pick-up was successful. Two days later, VA-145 flew in response to a downed VA-15 A-4C pilot, but Lt P C Craig could not be located – had been killed in the crash of his aircraft.

On 7 July, Lt Cdr Ken Hassett and Lt(jg) N G 'Greg' Davis responded to the downing of an VMA-311 A-4E pilot who had spent the night inside the DMZ. The 'Spad' pilots located the Marine and Hassett sent Davis to escort the rescue helicopter. Hassett

The pilot of VA-145 A-1H BuNo 139820 spreads the aircraft's dive brakes for the benefit of the HU-16 crew it is escorting over the Tonkin Gulf in 1967 during the 'Swordsmen's' last Skyraider deployment to Vietnam. The three hydraulically-powered dive brakes – one on each side of the fuselage and one below – gave the A-1H/J good stability when it came to visually aiming bombs in steep dives (*Tom Hansen via Wayne Mutza collection*)

orbited away from the pilot's position to conceal his location while awaiting the helicopter. As the latter approached, the two 'Swordsmen' strafed enemy positions while the helicopter made the rescue. Hassett's A-1 took some hits, as did the helicopter, but all three aircraft returned safely.

VA-145's first non-RESCAP mission of the deployment came on 9 July, when CVW-10 destroyed artillery positions in North Vietnam that were pounding Marines south of the DMZ. A-1 pilots initially flew as FACs for the wing's A-4s, before attacking the positions themselves.

During a respite from the line, Cdr Walter J Schutz relieved Sparks as CO of the 'Swordsmen'. Returning to the Tonkin Gulf on 28 July, *Intrepid* provided relief to USS *Forrestal* (CVA-59), reeling from a devastating fire. The next day, four VA-145 pilots searched for crewmen who may have ended up in the water, but found none.

This line period began rather uneventfully, but ramped up to a number of SAR missions. Hassett and Davis launched on 7 August in response to the loss of a USAF F-4C, but the downed crew was captured. On 17 August, Alvarez and Bumgarner covered the successful extraction of an injured F-105 pilot from the Tonkin Gulf. Four days later, Lt Dave Maples and Lt(jg) Norm Lessard responded to a distress call from a VF-142 F-4B crew downed deep inside North Vietnam. They soon located the pilot, while Schutz and Lt(jg) Bruce D Page escorted a UH-2 to the pick-up. After 40 minutes, the other crewman was extracted too.

Alvarez and Bumgarner went inland on 26 August to the crash scene of a USAF F-100F near the coast north of the DMZ. They exhausted their ammunition by strafing and rocketing enemy gun positions and then headed home when Schutz and 'CAG-10', Cdr Ken Burrows, arrived, escorting the two HH-3Es. The rescue team lost communications with the two downed pilots, so the A-1s escorted the helicopter to a safer area.

The Skyraider pilots then suppressed enemy fire while the helicopter picked up Capt Corwin Kippenhan. One was hit by AAA, and both HH-3Es withdrew while the A-1s searched in vain for the other pilot, Maj George E 'Bud' Day (flying his 139th mission). The latter, who was badly injured, was captured but soon escaped and eluded captivity for almost two weeks, crossing into South Vietnam, where he was seized by the VC. Returned to North Vietnam, Day survived captivity and was awarded the Medal of Honor upon his release on 14 March 1973.

The next line period also started routinely, but on 3 October a VA-145 section consisting of Lt Cdr Mannie Hendrix and Lt(jg) Greg Davis became involved in the rescue attempt of an F-105D pilot 15 miles northeast of Haiphong. While en route, they received a report that a VFS-3 A-4B pilot was downed in Haiphong harbour. Hendrix diverted his section to the harbour and located the pilot, marking his position with a smoke marker. A UH-2 from HC-7 picked up the injured pilot and Hendrix and Davis escorted the helicopter to safety.

The rescue attempt for the F-105 pilot resumed early the next day, with the 'Swordsmen' sending a division, led by Schutz, to the scene. Voice contact was established with the pilot, who was unable to reveal his exact position because of his close proximity to the enemy. Schutz began a low-level search, making three passes while under heavy fire. On the third pass, his 'Spad' was hit in the canopy and one wing. He returned to the scene after assessing the damage to his A-1, but received another hit that caused the loss of hydraulic pressure. The rescue attempt was suspended because of the heavy flak.

Five 'Swordsmen', led by Hendrix, returned to the scene that afternoon. Hendrix and his wingman, Lt(jg) Dick Lee, encountered intense AAA and descended to low altitude as they established contact with the downed pilot. Having located his position, Lt Tom Dixon and Lessard escorted the UH-2 to the scene. The pilot fired his

last smoke signal but the helicopter crew failed to see it, so Hendrix dropped a smoke light to mark the position.

The helicopter then encountered heavy fire, forcing Hendrix to make strafing runs to draw fire away from the UH-2. His A-1 was duly hit in the fuselage, wings and drop tank, so he pulled away and called in a jet strike group to suppress the AAA. The UH-2 was also hit, and it headed for the coast while rapidly losing fuel. The helicopter ditched five miles south of Hon Gay, and its crew was rescued by an H-3 from HC-7. Further attempts to rescue the F-105 pilot were unsuccessful and he was captured.

Another rescue attempt also met with failure on 7 October. Schutz and Page had proceeded to the scene of a downed F-105 pilot in northern North Vietnam, locating a parachute on the ground and hearing a beeper signal. Alvarez and Davis, meanwhile, were also heading to this location with a UH-2 from the South SAR Station, but they were soon recalled. Schutz and Page eventually escorted a USAF HH-3E to the scene, but by then the parachute had been removed and the beeper signal lost.

On 8 November, Hassett and Bumgarner were conducting an armed reconnaissance mission along the coast of northern North Vietnam when they were diverted to a rescue attempt for the crew of an F-100F downed near Dong Hoi. Enemy forces were firing small arms, machine guns and mortars at the two USAF pilots in the water. Passes by the A-1s also kept enemy boats at bay until a HH-3E picked up the airmen.

Three days later, Hendrix and Lt Larry Pickett proceeded into Laos to assist in the rescue attempt of an F-4C crew that had been downed on the 9th. The two 'Swordsmen' joined a USAF A-1 ('Sandy 3') and an HH-3E. Another USAF Skyraider ('Sandy 1') directed jet strikes into the area southwest of the downed crew. AAA damaged the helicopter, forcing it to withdraw with 'Sandy 3' as an escort. 'Sandy 1', low on fuel, turned over on-scene commander duties to Hendrix. 'Sandy 3' then escorted another HH-3E to the scene, but it too was hit while over the downed pilot and withdrew. Hendrix also received hits in his wing at this time, and passed on-scene commander duties to 'Sandy 3'. Another USAF A-1 was shot down during the recovery attempt and its pilot also rescued.

By now running low on fuel, Hendrix and Pickett were diverted to Khe Sanh, where the prop wash from the aircraft shattered the airstrip's wooden runway and damaged the rudder of Hendrix's A-1. The pair were able to return to *Intrepid* the next morning.

The rescue attempt was ultimately unsuccessful, for the pilot of the F-4C (Lt Col J W Armstrong) was killed and severely injured 1Lt

The unofficial *Tonkin Gulf Yacht Club* emblem was applied to Skyraiders by some A-1 squadrons (specifically VA-145 and VA-165) late in the aircraft's US Navy career. The patch, showing a Vietnamese junk superimposed over the Republic of Vietnam's flag of gold with three horizontal red stripes, is shown here applied to VA-145's *BABY*, alias A-1J BuNo 142033 AK 501 at Da Nang AB in August 1967 (*Tom Hansen via Wayne Mutza collection*)

A close-up of the *Tonkin Gulf Yacht Club* emblem on VA-145 A-1J BuNo 142033 (*Tom Hansen via Wayne Mutza collection*)

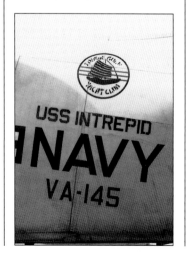

Lance Sijan was eventually captured after evading for six weeks. He subsequently died in captivity, and was posthumously awarded the Medal of Honor in March 1976.

During 102 days on the line, VA-145 assisted in the rescue of 14 pilots and expended 45,950 rounds of 20 mm ammunition, 25,587 2.75-in and 192 five-inch rockets and 300 250-lb bombs. Returning to Alameda on 30 December 1967, VA-145 moved to NAS Whidbey on 1 January 1968 for transition to the A-6A. It returned to Vietnam in January 1969.

## 'ACES' WILD

When VA-152, commanded by Cdr D M Willson, returned to *Yankee Station* on board *Oriskany* on 14 July 1967, 'the complexion of the war had changed', in the words of the unit historian. The emphasis had shifted from the armed reconnaissance of the lower route packages of southern North Vietnam to the bombing of key targets in the Northeast Triangle – Hanoi, Haiphong and the northeast railway line. The heavy air defences in the latter region precluded A-1 operations overland, except in the SAR role and when accompanied by jet aircraft.

On its first day back on the line, VA-152 concentrated its attention on WBLCs along the coast of North Vietnam. The 'Spads' destroyed ten vessels that day, but a price was exacted on 15 July when Lt(jg) Robin B Cassell was killed (in A-1H BuNo 135288) by AAA from Hon Ne during an armed reconnaissance mission along the North Vietnamese coast.

The heavy strikes north of the DMZ that characterised the summer of 1967 provided the unit with a steady supply of SAR opportunities. The first of these occurred on 16 July, when a section led by XO Cdr A B Headley provided cover for a downed VF-162 F-8 pilot near Phu Ly until nightfall. The following day, a four-aeroplane division of A-1s was able to lead a Sea King in to rescue the pilot. Another SAR mission was flown on 18 July by four VA-152 pilots, and they were joined by several VA-215 A-1s. The aircraft flew in to cover two VA-164 A-4 pilots that had been downed near Phu Ly. One was rescued by a USAF HH-3, but ground fire critically wounded a crewman on a US Navy SH-3 Sea King, which had to withdraw. A UH-2 launched to replace it also took hits and withdrew.

The rescue operation continued the next day when Willson led six VA-152 Skyraiders as escorts for yet another SH-3. This time the RESCAP was also covered by A-4s. While the Skyraiders marked the downed pilot's position with Zuni rockets, a cluster bomb dropped by an A-4 failed to open and exploded near the pilot. The Sea King's crew mistook the cluster bomb for a Zuni and flew over flak guns in the valley. The helicopter went down in flames with all hands. 'Spads' escorted another helicopter into the area, but the effort was discontinued without a successful pick-up.

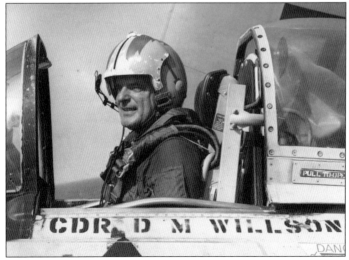

Cdr D M Willson led the 'Wild Aces' into combat during VA-152's third Vietnam Skyraider deployment in 1967-68. Willson is wearing a single-visor helmet with a boom microphone. His A-1 is equipped with the Yankee rocket extraction system. The Skyraiders of VA-152 and VA-25 were fitted with the system during their last deployments. Only one US Navy pilot, Lt(jg) Joseph Dunn of VA-25, had occasion to use it when his A-1H was shot down near Hainan Island by two Chinese MiG-17s on 14 February 1968. A VAW-13 EA-1F crew in company with Dunn reported seeing an ejection, but the pilot was declared missing (*US Navy/PH3 Wohler*)

On 20 July, two VA-152 pilots escorted a UH-2 in a successful rescue of a VA-212 A-4 pilot who had come down amongst a group of islands near the Chinese border. The remainder of the month was relatively unexciting, although the squadron did destroy 16 WBLCs. On 28 July, Lt Cdr J O Harmon and Lt(jg) R L Lindsay also sank a PT boat east of Haiphong. Four days later six VA-152 pilots escorted a UH-2 for a successful pick-up of an A-4 pilot east of Haiphong. That same day Harmon and Lt(jg) A L Langlinais destroyed a PT boat, repeating the feat on 4 August.

VA-152 also spotted for naval vessels shelling coastal targets as part of *Sea Dragon*. During a typical mission, if the ships drew no return fire, the 'Spads' were released to perform coastal armed reconnaissance.

During this deployment, VA-152's Lt Jack Baker also earned the distinction of flying the last tanker sortie in a Skyraider – an unsung role performed without fuss by all A-1 units.

The intensity of *Rolling Thunder* raids in the Northeast Triangle increased in August 1967. The lack of terrain suitable for evasion and the heavy air defences throughout this area precluded most SAR operations. However, on 26 August Willson and Lt(jg) J D Ward covered the successful rescue of a USAF F-4 pilot just north of the DMZ.

Some 30 WBLCs were also destroyed by VA-152 in August-September, followed by 64 in October and 21 in November-December. A three-aircraft detachment operated from Chul Lai, in South Vietnam, for three weeks in October for naval gunfire spotting. No more SAR missions were conducted in the last two months of the cruise, and the deployment ended quietly. VA-152 returned home on 31 January 1968 and began transitioning to the A-4B. The unit would return once more to *Yankee Station* in 1970, flying A-4Es.

A VA-152 A-1 is spotted on the flightdeck of CVA-34 in December 1967. The oily grime covering its wing surfaces is a normal feature of carrier operations. Oil, fuel, grease and hydraulic fluid made for a grimy mixture that was walked all over carrier aircraft by personnel climbing onto them for maintenance and servicing (*US Navy/PH3 C B Vesper via Robert F Dorr collection*)

*Oriskany* steams in the South China Sea on 3 January 1968. On its starboard forward quarter are five A-1s of VA-152 and two EA-1Fs of VAW-13 (*US Navy/PHC Neal Crowe*)

## 'SPAD' FINALE FOR THE 'FIST'

VA-25, with Cdr James D Burden as CO, transferred from CVW-2 to CVW-15 on 1 April 1967, but it stayed with *Coral Sea* for the squadron's third Vietnam deployment. On 9 June, Rear Adm Fred E Bakutis, Commander, Fleet Air Alameda, joined the squadron in a

tribute to the A-1 Skyraider, which it had flown since 21 September 1947. Also attending the ceremony were the Skyraider's designers, Ed Heinemann and L J Devlin of the Douglas Aircraft Company.

*Coral Sea* deployed on 26 July 1967 for the Skyraider's last combat cruise with an attack squadron. The carrier carried no fewer than 16 A-1H/Js, four of which were off-loaded at NAF Atsugi, Japan, as spares. Things did not get off to a good start, however, for on 19 August, while conducting practice strikes off Okinawa, Lt Cdr Frederick H Gates was killed when his A-1H (BuNo 137575) suffered engine failure while on approach to the carrier and crashed into the sea.

VA-25 began RESCAP and *Sea Dragon* sorties off North Vietnam on 28 August. Two days later, another engine failure caused by AAA resulted in the ditching of the A-1H (BuNo 135390) flown by Lt(jg) Larry E Gardiner. Having made an attacking pass on logistics boats near Cape Falaise, 30 miles north of Vinh, Gardiner was about to fire off his rockets when his 'Spad' was hit and he was forced to ditch. Five of his squadron-mates silenced the AAA batteries, allowing the downed pilot to be rescued by a USAF HH-3E before he could be seized by an enemy patrol boat.

On 7 September, VA-25 assisted US Navy ships in knocking out several shore batteries that had been firing on them. Four days later, two 'Fist' pilots launched on a night SAR mission north of the DMZ. Lt Cdr Carter Moser turned on his lights to mark the position of the rescue helicopter to the downed pilot, who in turn fired a flare to denote his location. However, he could not be recovered. The line period ended on 27 September when four A-1s destroyed 12 bunkers and uncovered a tunnel in the DMZ. On 1 October Cdr Clifford E Church relieved Burden as CO of VA-25. While resting at Subic Bay, new electronic countermeasures equipment in the form of ALE-29 chaff dispensers and APR-27 radar warning receivers was installed in the squadron's aircraft.

*Coral Sea* returned to *Yankee Station* on 11 October for two weeks. Three days later, Lt Cdr Ralph Smith and Lt Cdr Ron Bolt observed a VAP-61 RA-3B on fire heading for the Tonkin Gulf. The aircraft eventually crashed into the sea six miles offshore, killing the pilot. Two crewmen had bailed out, how-ever, and they entered the water in the middle of a North Vietnamese fishing fleet. The 'Spads' conducted six rocket and strafing runs, sinking six boats and diverting the rest away from the two crewmen, who then came under fire from shore batter-ies. As two A-4s attacked the latter,

VA-152 A-1H BuNo 134575 *FOO FOO JUICE* is shown parked on an apron in March 1968 at the Naval Air Rework Facility (NARF) at NAS Quonset Point, Rhode Island, after retirement following the completion of the unit's last deployment with the Skyraider. Note that the A-1's four 20 mm cannon have already been removed. The NARF overhauled Skyraiders for the US Navy, and also processed them for transfer to the USAF and VNAF. Administratively stricken for transfer to the USAF, this aircraft was supplied to the VNAF and eventually lost in combat on 21 June 1974 (*Wayne Mutza collection*)

VA-25 A-1H BuNo 134589 is framed by the armament of another 'Fist' 'Spad' during a mission over the Tonkin Gulf. The two 20 mm cannon in each wing were useful for strafing during close air support and rescue missions. The tips of four 5-inch Zuni rockets can also be seen protruding from an LAU-10 launcher at lower right (*Rosario Rausa via Peter Mersky collection*)

VA-25 A-1J BuNo 142077 taxis along the flightdeck of *Coral Sea* after trapping back aboard at the end of yet another mission over Southeast Asia. As indicated by the black cordite residue on the underside of the folding wing behind the starboard outer 20 mm cannon, this aircraft had been using its guns in a strafing role during the course of the sortie (*US Navy*)

As if in hand-off, a section of VA-25 Skyraiders leads a section of A-7A Corsair IIs assigned to VA-147 over the Tonkin Gulf on 23 January 1968, a month before *Coral Sea* departed *Yankee Station* for home at the completion of the third Vietnam deployment for both ship and squadron. VA-147 took the A-7 on its first deployment in late 1967 on board *Ranger*. Of the ten A-1 attack squadrons that served in the Vietnam War, the Skyraider was replaced by the A-6A in six of them (VA-52, -115, -145, -165, -176 and -196), the A-4 in two squadrons (VA-95 and -152) and the A-7 in one squadron (VA-25). VA-215 was disestablished, but a second VA-215, flying A-7Bs, was later established and carried on the 'Barn Owl' traditions (*US Navy/PH1 Jean C Cote*)

Smith directed in a UH-2, which plucked the crewmen to safety.

On 24 October, four A-1 pilots helped rescue an F-105 pilot two miles south of Do Son Peninsula. Lt Cdr Rosario M 'Zip' Rausa and Bolt responded to the incident, covering the pilot until he was rescued by an HH-3A from HC-7. CVA-43 left *Yankee Station* four days later and returned to Subic Bay, where all 12 of VA-25's A-1s had the Stanley Aviation Yankee rocket extraction seat installed as the first fleet unit to be fitted with the escape system.

On 4 December, two VA-25 pilots came to the assistance of a destroyer that had been hit by shore batteries north of Cape Mui Ron. Guided by two S-2 Tracker aircraft, the A-1s took out the enemy batteries. Eighteen days later, VA-25 pilots responded to two SAR calls. Four of them located VA-155 A-4E pilot Lt Cdr Wilmer Cook who had been shot down near Ha Tinh. Finding him face down in a rice paddy, the 'Spads' vectored the rescue helicopter to his location, and it hovered a few feet over the pilot. Confirming that he was dead, the helicopter crew departed under heavy fire. A large number of enemy troops were then cut down during strafing passes by the 'Spads', two of which received hits from small arms.

Two other A-1s from VA-25 encountered heavy flak later that day while searching for VA-147 A-7A pilot Lt Cdr James Hickerson, who was taken prisoner before he could be located by the rescue team. Hickerson's Corsair II was the first example of its type to be lost in combat.

On 26 December, two VA-25 Skyraiders sank ten WBLCS. One of the 'Spads', flown by Lt(jg) Bruce Marcus, was hit in the propeller and windscreen by 12.7 mm rounds, but the pilot returned unscathed.

Two more SAR missions were flown by VA-25 before year end. A pair of A-1s on a *Sea Dragon* mission on 27 December responded to a mayday call from an F-4C 15 miles off the coast near Dong Ha. The 'Spad' pilots witnessed the water impact and located the downed pilots. Unfortunately, one of the pilots slipped from the SAR helicopter's sling at the door and was never found again. On 29 December, four A-1s covered the rescue of the crew of a VF-161 F-4B from the water near Cam Pha.

The Tet Offensive, launched in January 1968 by the VC and North Vietnamese Army, engaged the attention of VA-25, which flew numerous close air support sorties in northern South Vietnam. When the Marine

Lt Bruce Marcus of VA-25 examines the hole in a propeller blade of his A-1 caused by a 12.7 mm machine gun. The rugged Skyraider had a reputation for being able to absorb considerable damage. Many made it back to a carrier or divert field, although some were too damaged to fly again. Most of the 49 US Navy Skyraiders downed in Southeast Asia fell victim to large calibre automatic cannon fire (*Rosario Rausa via Peter Mersky collection*)

The pilot of 'Canasta 414' *NORTH VIETNAMESE CROP DUSTER*, alias A-1J BuNo 142070 of VA-25 during the squadron's last Skyraider deployment, is strapped in by his plane captain on the flightdeck of CVA-43. The four tips of the 5-in Zuni rockets are seen protruding from the LAU-10 launchers on the inboard stations beneath both wings (*US Navy via Wayne Mutza collection*)

Corps firebase at Khe Sanh came under siege, the unit joined the aerial onslaught that broke the siege – details of its participation in this legendary action are contained in the caption for the cover artwork.

VA-25 was to suffer one more loss before returning home. On 14 February, Lt(jg) Joseph P Dunn was ferrying an A-1H (BuNo 134499) from Cubi Point to *Coral Sea* in company with a VAW-13 EA-1F. The section drifted off course as they headed north and flew near the east coast of Hainan Island, where they were intercepted by two communist Chinese MiG-17s. Dunn's 'Spad' was hit and crashed seven miles offshore from the village of Kao-lung. The EA-1F crew saw Dunn deploy his parachute (his aircraft was equipped with a Stanley Aviation extraction seat) and headed for Da Nang. A SAR effort was misdirected toward North Vietnam before the course error was realised, however, and although a beeper was heard near Hainan during a sweep eight hours after he had been downed, no sign of Dunn was ever found.

On 20 February 1968, VA-25 flew its last combat sorties of the deployment against the artillery sites around Khe Sanh. Cdr Church's wingman, Lt(jg) Theodore 'Ted' Hill Jr – appropriately, the very last Skyraider student pilot to graduate from VA-122 – brought A-1H BuNo 135300 NE 405 home to *Coral Sea* for its final landing from a combat mission, closing out the frontline career of the US Navy's attack versions of the 'Spad'. CVA-43 left the Tonkin Gulf and returned to Alameda on 6 April 1968. Four days later, VA-25 hosted a farewell ceremony for the A-1 at Lemoore. Hill started up the engine of BuNo 135300, taxied between rows of saluting sideboys, and took off, making a farewell pass. The A-1H was subsequently delivered to the Naval Aviation Museum at NAS Pensacola, Florida, for permanent display. VA-25 would return to Vietnam as an A-7B Corsair II squadron in February 1969.

## END OF AN ERA

In a seemingly odd development, VA-176 was chosen to return to its familiar operating area, the Mediterranean, in June 1967. Until this time, almost two years had elapsed since attack A-1s had deployed on board a Mediterranean-bound carrier. When USS *Saratoga* (CVA-60) departed Mayport, Florida, on 2 May 1967, it carried only two attack squadrons – a reflection of the demands the conflict in Vietnam was placing on US naval aviation. VA-216, equipped with A-4Bs, joined VA-176, which, in order to compensate for the lack of a third attack squadron in CVW-3, was equipped with no fewer than 20 A-1H/Js – rather than 12, as per usual – flown by 26 pilots.

What had promised to be a laid-back cruise quickly changed when, on 8 June 1967, the US Navy intel-ligence-gathering ship USS *Liberty* (AGTR-5) was attacked by Israeli aircraft and torpedo boats during the June 1967 Arab-Israeli War. Four 'Spads' from VA-176, armed

with Zuni rockets and flares, were launched from CVA-60 to defend *Liberty*, but they were recalled before they engaged any attackers.

Cdr J T French relieved Cdr A R Ashworth as CO of VA-176 on 1 August 1967. The unit lost two 'Spads' to mishaps during the deployment. Lt(jg) C M Dashiell's A-1H (BuNo 135294) developed an engine fire on 24 June 1967 and he was rescued after baling out over the Mediterranean. On 7 August,

Lt R G Foster's A-1H (BuNo 139792) also suffered an engine fire, forcing the pilot to take to his parachute near Sigonella, Sicily – he was rescued without injury. VA-176 returned home from the last Mediterranean attack A-1 cruise on 6 December 1967.

For all of the fanfare at Lemoore, VA-25 was not, technically, the last US Navy attack squadron to operate the A-1. Fifteen days after this event, on 25 April 1968, VA-176 held a change-of-command ceremony at its NAS Jacksonville home. As Cdr C L Cook relieved Cdr J T French, the 'Thunderbolts' simultaneously retired the last of their attack A-1s. Two A-1Hs, parked on either side of an A-6A – VA-176's future – started their engines, taxied to the active runway, took off and flew by the gathered crowd in a final salute to the 'Spad'. VA-176 moved to Oceana the following month to begin its transition to the Intruder.

The 'Electric Spad', however, had almost two more years of frontline life left in it, but it was winding down rapidly. The EKA-3B Skywarrior, which began its first deployment with VAW-13 in November 1967, was ready to step in as successor to the EA-1F. However, the squadron was short of 'Whales', so *Kitty Hawk* and CVW-11 took the EA-1Fs of VAW-13's Det 63 on deployment to the Tonkin Gulf on 18 November 1967, returning on 28 June 1968.

VA-25's Lt(jg) Theodore 'Ted' Hill, who flew the last US Navy attack A-1 mission of the Vietnam War in this A-1H BuNo 135300 NL 405, revs the engine in preparation for take-off from NAS Lemoore on 10 April 1968 during a retirement ceremony for the aircraft. Hill was also the last graduate of the A-1 curriculum at VA-122 prior to the squadron switching to training pilots for the A-7. After take-off, Hill made a low pass in salute to the gathered crowd, before heading to NAS Pensacola, Florida, where the 'Spad' was put on display in the Naval Aviation Museum, now the National Museum of Naval Aviation (*Harry Gann via Robert F Dorr collection*)

Two VA-176 A-1Hs loaded with 25-lb practice bombs line up on the waist catapults of CVA-60 in 1967 during the squadron's last deployment with Skyraiders (*MAP*)

A VAW-13 EA-1F traps on board *Kitty Hawk* on 17 April 1968. This VAW-13 detachment deployed with CVA-63 from NAS Alameda, California, as the squadron's Det 1 was winding down operations at NAS Cubi Point, in the Philippines (*US Navy/PH3 G S Brown via Robert F Dorr collection*)

Flightdeck crewmen rig a VAW-33 EA-1F to a catapult for launch from *Intrepid* on 18 September 1967 in the Tonkin Gulf. VAW-33's detachment with CVW-10 for its second Vietnam deployment was the first of three supplied by the Atlantic Fleet's carrier-based electronic jamming squadron. This aircraft is equipped with a centreline Aero 1C 300-gallon external tank, an APS-31C search radar under the starboard wing, a chaff dispensing pod under the port wing and ALT-2 or -7 jamming pods under each outboard wing (*US Navy/PH3 R A Lucas*)

VAW-13 Det 1 shut down its activities at Cubi Point six weeks later, with ceremonies being held on 10 August 1968. VAW-13 was finally redesignated Tactical Electronic Warfare Squadron 130 (VAQ-130) on 1 October 1968, its name now truly reflecting its mission. The unit retained a dual-control A-1E (BuNo 132446, which had been returned to the US Navy after being modified for the USAF) for a year as a 'hack', and it proved to be particularly useful for flying A-3 tyres out to VAQ-130 detachments conducting carrier qualifications off the coast of California.

VAQ-33 (redesignated from VAW-33 on 1 February 1968) would send three more EA-1F dets on deployment during the last two years of the 'Spad's' fleet service. VAQ-33 Det 14 deployed to the Tonkin Gulf with CVW-19 on West Coast carrier *Ticonderoga* from December 1967 through to August 1968. The 'Knight Hawk's' Det 11 took the EA-1F on its last combat deployment as part of CVW-10, which in turn embarked in *Intrepid* for the carrier's final Vietnam War cruise in June 1968. The EA-1F's last combat mission was flown on 27 December 1968.

The 'Spad's' last deployment would not return it to war, but on a cruise to the Mediterranean, beginning on 5 April 1969 with CVW-1 on board USS *John F Kennedy* (CVA-67). VAQ-33 Det 67 lost an aircraft (BuNo 132599) to a mishap on 28 June, but its crew was rescued. The unit's last two EA-1Fs (BuNos 132506 and 132575) flew off on 20 December 1969, ending the operational career of the Skyraider in US Navy service.

The four A-1s that had served for years as flying laboratories and test aircraft had also been phased out by mid-1971. An NA-1G (BuNo 132598) assigned to the Naval Weapons Center China Lake, California, was transferred to the USAF, and an EA-1F (BuNo 132532) with the Naval Air Test Center (NATC) Patuxent River, Maryland, was donated to the Naval Aviation Museum. An EA-1E (BuNo 135178) used for aeromedical research at the Naval Aeromedical Institute at NAS Pensacola, Florida, was donated to the Marine Corps museum, but it was later acquired by a private owner and still flies at US airshows today.

The US Navy's last 'Spad', NA-1E BuNo 132443, which had served for ten years at NATC as an ordnance, avionics and carrier suitability test platform, was retired on 7 July 1971. Cdr C B Niedhold flew it to the Confederate Air Force Museum in Harlingen, Texas, for display as a static exhibit. It too has survived the past 38 years, the aircraft presently residing in the Texas Air Museum in Hondo, Texas.

# APPENDICES

## APPENDIX A

### A-1 SQUADRON CARRIER DEPLOYMENTS 1964-68

| Squadron | Nickname | Call sign | Aircraft | Tail code | Modex | Air Wing | Carrier | Deployment Dates |
|---|---|---|---|---|---|---|---|---|
| VA-25 | 'Fist of the Fleet' | 'Canasta' | A-1H/J | NE | 570-581 | CVW-2 | CVA-41 | 6 Mar 65 to 23 Nov 65 |
| | | | A-1H/J | NE | 571-582 | CVW-2 | CVA-43 | 29 Jul 66 to 23 Feb 67 |
| | | | A-1H/J | NL | 401-414 | CVW-15 | CVA-43 | 26 Jul 67 to 6 Apr 68 |
| VA-52 | 'Knightriders' | 'Viceroy' | A-1H/J | NF | 300-311 | CVW-5 | CVA-14 | 14 Apr 64 to 15 Dec 64 |
| | | | A-1H/J | NF | 300-311 | CVW-5 | CVA-14 | 28 Sep 65 to 13 May 66 |
| | | | A-1H/J | NM | 300-311 | CVW-19 | CVA-14 | 15 Oct 66 to 29 May 67 |
| VA-95 | 'Skyknights' | 'Green Lizard'/ | A-1H/J | NG | 500-511 | CVW-9 | CVA-61 | 5 Aug 64 to 6 May 65 |
| | | 'Fortress' | | | | | | |
| VA-115 | 'Arabs' | 'Arab' | A-1H/J | NH | 501-513 | CVW-11 | CVA-63 | 17 Oct 63 to 20 Jul 64 |
| | | | A-1H/J | NH | 500-513 | CVW-11 | CVA-63 | 19 Oct 65 to 13 Jun 66 |
| | | | A-1H/J | NF | 500-513 | CVW-5 | CVA-19 | 5 Jan 67 to 22 Jul 67 |
| VA-145 | 'Swordsmen' | 'Electron' | A-1H/J | NK | 500-513 | CVW-14 | CVA-64 | 5 May 64 to 1 Feb 65 |
| | | | A-1H/J | NK | 501-514 | CVW-14 | CVA-61 | 10 Dec 65 to 25 Aug 66 |
| | | | A-1H/J | AK | 500-511 | CVW-10 | CVS-11 | 11 May 67 to 30 Dec 67 |
| VA-152 | 'Wild Aces' | 'Locket' | A-1H/J | AH | 581-592 | CVW-16 | CVA-34 | 5 Apr 65 to 16 Dec 65 |
| | | | A-1H/J | AH | 500-511 | CVW-16 | CVA-34 | 26 May 66 to 16 Nov 66 |
| | | | A-1H/J | AH | 500-512 | CVW-16 | CVA-34 | 16 Jun 67 to 31 Jan 68 |
| VA-165 | 'Boomers' | Firewood | A-1H/J | AH | 581-592 | CVW-16 | CVA-34 | 1 Aug 63 to 10 Mar 64 |
| | | | A-1H/J | NL | 200-212 | CVW-15 | CVA-43 | 7 Dec 64 to 1 Nov 65 |
| | | | A-1H/J | AK | 200-211 | CVW-10 | CVS-11 | 4 Apr 66 to 21 Nov 66 |
| VA-176 | 'Thunderbolts' | 'Papoose' | A-1H/J | AK | 400-412 | CVW-10 | CVS-11 | 4 Apr 66 to 21 Nov 66 |
| VA-196 | 'Main Battery' | 'Milestone' | A-1H/J | NM | 600-612 | CVW-19 | CVA-31 | 28 Jan 64 to 21 Nov 64 |
| | | | A-1H/J | NM | 600-612 | CVW-19 | CVA-31 | 21 Apr 65 to 13 Jan 66 |
| VA-215 | 'Barn Owls' | 'Barn Owl' | A-1H/J | NP | 560-571 | CVW-21 | CVA-19 | 21 Oct 64 to 29 May 65 |
| | | | A-1H/J | NP | 560-571 | CVW-21 | CVA-19 | 10 Nov 65 to 1 Aug 66 |
| | | | A-1H/J | NP | 560-571 | CVW-21 | CVA-31 | 29 Jan 67 to 25 Aug 67 |
| VAW-33 Det 11 'Knight Hawks' | | 'Snowshoe' | EA-1F | AK | 601-603 | CVW-10 | CVS-11 | 11 May 67 to 30 Dec 67 |
| VAQ-33 Det 14 | | | EA-1F | NM | 704-706 | CVW-19 | CVA-14 | 27 Dec 67 to 17 Aug 68 |
| VAQ-33 Det 11 | | | EA-1F | AK | 801-803 | CVW-10 | CVS-11 | 4 Jun 68 to 8 Feb 69 |
| VAW-13 Det 1 'Zappers' | | 'Robbie' | EA-1F | VR | Note | Various | Various | Various |
| VAW-13 Det 63 | | | EA-1F | VR | 011-013 | CVW-11 | CVA-63 | 18 Nov 67 to 28 Jun 68 |
| VAW-11 Det Q 'Early Eleven' | | 'Overpass' | EA-1E | RR | 71-73 | CVSG-59 | CVS-20 | 20 Feb 64 to 11 Aug 64 |
| VAW-11 Det R | | | EA-1E | RR | 700-703 | CVSG-53 | CVS-33 | 19 Jun 64 to 16 Dec 64 |
| VAW-11 Det T | | | EA-1E | RR | 710-715 | CVSG-55 | CVS-10 | 23 Oct 64 to 16 May 65 |

**Note:** Most VAW-13 EA-1F detachments until 1 October 1968 were despatched from VAW-13 Det 1 at NAS Cubi Point, in the Philippines, and frequently rotated between carriers as they arrived and departed the line. Some of these dets carried temporary designations, but it is not known if they were official. Modexes in the 7XX series were used initially. Later, Det 1 used modex series 77X-78X.

# APPENDIX B

## VIETNAM-ERA US NAVY A-1 TYPES IN SERVICE

Four models of Skyraider saw service with the US Navy during the conflict in Southeast Asia, namely the the EA-1E, EA-1F, A-1H and A-1J.

**EA-1E –** The EA-1E (AD-5W), a four-seat radar early warning version of the A-1E, was being phased out during the early 1960s in favour of the Grumman E-1B. Tracer. By 1964 the EA-1E – operated by VAW-11 – served only in detachments on Pacific Fleet CVSs. EA-1Es, equipped with the APS-20 radar, deployed to Vietnam on board *Bennington*, *Kearsarge* and *Yorktown* in 1964 and 1965 before they were retired.

**EA-1F –** The EA-1F (AD-5Q) was a four-seat elec-tronic countermeasures conversion of the A-1G (AD-5N) night-attack variant. Initially, a total of 58 were converted from A-1Gs using kits. A further six were converted from EA-1Es by Naval Air Rework Facility Quonset Point, Rhode Island, in 1966 to compensate for attrition and heavy use in South-east Asia. These six aircraft, benefiting from newer technology and the removal of obsolete wiring and systems, were lighter that the original EA-1Fs and more popular among the pilots that flew them. EA-1Fs were operated from bases in Vietnam for *Waterglass* operations and over Southeast Asia by three-aeroplane detachments on board carriers from VAW-13 and VAW-33 (later VAQ-33). The EA-1F jammed enemy radars and dropped chaff to pro-tect attacking aircraft. Only one was lost to enemy action. The EA-1F was the last US Navy version to see combat over Vietnam and to see operational service in the fleet. VAW-13 had replaced its EA-1Fs with EKA-3B Skywarriors by October 1968, and the

aircraft was retired by VAQ-33 in December 1969. One EA-1F subsequently remained in operation for a year undertaking test work at NAS Patuxent River.

**A-1H –** The single-seat A-1H (AD-6), a refinement of the AD-4B, became the definitive production attack variant of the Skyraider. Douglas Aircraft built a total of 712 A-1Hs, and they had rapidly replaced earlier versions in attack squadrons by the late 1950s. The A-1H had a nuclear-attack capability, a role belied by its anachronistic appearance on carrier decks, but enhanced by its long range. A mainstay of US Navy Skyraider-equipped VA squadrons serving in Southeast Asia, the A-1H was finally withdrawn from fleet service on 25 April 1968. In 1967, remaining A-1Hs in VA-25 and VA-152 were equipped with Stanley Aviation Yankee rocket-extraction systems for the pilots.

**A-1J –** The last production version of the Skyraider, the A-1J (AD-7) differed from the A-1H in being equipped with a strengthened centre section and beefed up landing gear, as well as the –26WB version of the R-3350 engine. The 72 A-1Js built were initially delivered in batches to three VA squadrons, but their similarity to A-1Hs eventually eliminated their segregation. Soon, A-1Js were mixed at random with A-1Hs in VA squadrons. Some were also equipped with the Stanley extraction seat in 1967. By mid-1968, all surviving A-1H/Js had been trans-ferred to Southeast Asia for USAF and VNAF service. Smaller numbers of several other versions served in training, logistics, and test work in the United States during the Vietnam War, including the **A-1E**, **NA-1E**, **UA-1E** and **NA-1G**.

# APPENDIX C

## A-1 ORDNANCE AND EXTERNAL STORES

The A-1 was famous for the heavy ordnance loads it carried into combat on its 15 stores stations. During the Vietnam War, US Navy A-1s rarely boasted the wide range of exotic ordnance that USAF Skyraiders employed in combat in part because of shipboard storage and handling restrictions.

All A-1H/Js were armed with four M3 20 mm cannon, each of which fired at a rate of 600 rounds per minute. A total of 800 rounds was carried. VA-25, for example, belted its 20 mm ammunition in the following order – armour-piercing tracer, high explosive, high explosive, armor-piercing incendiary, armour-piercing incendiary. Flash hiders were often installed on the gun barrels for night operations. EA-1Fs in the combat zone were armed with two cannon installed in the inboard wing sections.

For attack missions US Navy A-1s typically carried general-purpose high-explosive 'dumb' bombs. Early in the war, the US Navy was running through its remaining stocks of World War 2-vintage high-drag box-finned bombs, mostly in 250-, 500-, 1000- and 2000-lb categories. As the war progressed, A-1s carried 750-lb M117 low-drag bombs and eventually the Mk 80 series of low-drag bombs – 250-lb Mk 81, 500-lb Mk 82, 1000-lb Mk 83 and 2000-lb Mk 84. Mk 81s and 82s were often fitted with Snakeye fins for low-altitude drops. On occasion, Mk 54 350-lb depth bombs were used in ground-attack missions. Bombs were also fitted with 'Daisy Cutter' fuse-extenders to explode above ground. Rockets were also widely used by US Navy A-1 squadrons. Single 5-in High-Velocity Aircraft

Rockets were phased out in early 1967 by four-shot LAU-10 Aero-7B pods of 5-in Zuni rockets. A common configuration for an A-1 – particularly while on RESCAP patrol – included one of these pods on each main wing station, as well as a 300-gallon Aero 1 centreline fuel tank.

Nineteen-shot LAU-60A pods of 2.75-in Mighty Mouse rockets – often mounted on the Aero 14 outboard wing stations – also were also used.

Mk 24 flares were also routinely dropped at night.

Other armaments less frequently used were Mk 77 Mod 0 750-lb, Mk 77 Mod 1 550-lb and Mk 79 1000-lb napalm fire bombs.

At least one commode was also dropped by a VA-25 A-1 on an enemy position.

External fuel tanks were normally carried for all missions in the combat zone. Two Aero 1 300-gallon tanks mounted on the inboard wing stations was a common configuration, although later in the war the carriage of a single 300-gallon tank on the centreline station became more the norm. EA-1Fs normally carried one Aero 1B 300-gallon tank, mounted on the centreline station.

The EA-1F could carry two pod-mounted radars – the ground-mapping APS-31 and the air-intercept APS-19, although the latter was carried less often. Typical mission loads included a 300-gallon Aero 1B centreline fuel tank and a mixture of up to four ALT-2 or -7 jamming pods or ALE-2 and MX-900 chaff-dispensing pods. Two 20 mm cannon were mounted in the wings.

The A-1 was capable of refuelling a jet aircraft using a buddy store. This capability was used in the Vietnam War, but not widely, mostly because of the availability by this time of A-3B and KA-3B Skywarriors with tanker packages.

# COLOUR PLATES

## 1
### A-1H BuNo 139662/NK 510 of VA-145, USS *Constellation* (CVA-64), August 1964
VA-145's only A-1 deployment on board CVA-64 saw the 'Swordsmen' flying the first US Navy strikes into North Vietnam in support of Operation *Pierce Arrow* on 5 August 1964. BuNo 139662 saw action in these early missions. Delivered to the US Navy as an AD-6 in November 1955, it duly served with VA-195 (1956-58), VA-196 (1959-60) and VA-115 (1961-63). The A-1 joined VA-145 in September 1963, and remained with the unit until May 1965. Stricken and transferred to the USAF two months later, it was supplied to the VNAF.

## 2
### A-1H BuNo 134569/NF 311 of VA-52, USS *Ticonderoga* (CVA-14), August 1964
This aircraft also participated in the *Pierce Arrow* strikes. Delivered to the US Navy in December 1953, it served with VF-194 (1954), VA-155 (1954-55), VA-125 (1956-57), VA-52 (1964-65), VA-122 (1965) and VA-52 once again, joining the unit as an attrition replacement aboard CVA-14 in the Tonkin Gulf in March 1966. It also participated in the unit's final A-1 combat cruise in 1966-67, before transferring to VA-152 aboard CVA-34 in the Tonkin Gulf in July 1967, and returned with the unit to CONUS in February 1968. Stricken for transfer to the USAF that same month, BuNo 134569 was passed on to the VNAF and lost in combat on 24 October 1972.

## 3
### EA-1E BuNo 133772/RR 73 of VAW-11 Det R, USS *Kearsarge* (CVS-33), September 1964
VAW-11 deployed three detachments of EA-1Es on board ASW carriers in the Tonkin Gulf prior to them being superseded by E-1B Tracers in 1965-66. This particular aircraft was delivered to the US Navy as an AD-5W in June 1955, and it served with Marine Corps unit VMC/VMCJ-3 (1955-56) and VC-11 (1956-57), prior to joining VAW-11 in 1958. BuNo 133772 was transferred to VAW-33 in March 1965 and assigned to the unit's Det 39. Embarked in USS *Lake Champlain* (CVS-39), the aircraft was written off in a flying accident at sea on 20 May 1965.

## 4
### A-1H BuNo 139715/NM 605 of VA-196, USS *Bon Homme Richard* (CVA-31), September 1964
This A-1 flew *Yankee Team* strikes into Laos between 31 August and 8 October 1964. Delivered to the US Navy in March 1956, BuNo 139715 was flown by VA-176 (1956-57), VA-16 (1957), VA-15 (1958-59), VA-122 (1960-61) and VA-196 (1961-65). It was administratively stricken for transfer to the USAF in July 1965 and handed over to the VNAF.

## 5
### A-1H BuNo 139779/NG 512 of VA-95, USS *Ranger* (CVA-61), March 1965
VA-95 made only one deployment to Vietnam with A-1s, and participated in *Flaming Dart*-the initial months of *Rolling Thunder*. BuNo 139779 was accepted by the US Navy in January 1956 and flown by VA-15 (1956-57), VA-45 (1957-58), the Marine Corps' Aircraft Engineering Squadron 12 (1958-60), VA-152 (1961-62), VA-115 (1962-63), and VA-196 (1964-65). It joined VA-95 as an attrition replacement for A-1H BuNo 135375 in March 1965 and was then transferred back to VA-196 in August 1965, but was passed on to VA-165 the following month. Issued to VA-25 in June 1966, it saw combat with the unit later that year, prior to joining VA-152 in April 1967. Another Vietnam cruise followed until 31 January 1968. Two weeks later, BuNo 135375 was transferred to the USAF and then the VNAF.

## 6
### A-1H BuNo 139770/NP 565 of VA-215, USS *Hancock* (CVA-19), April 1965
This aircraft saw combat with VA-215 in *Flaming Dart* and early *Rolling Thunder* strikes. Delivered in June 1956, it served with VA-15 (1956), VA-35

(1957), VA-42 (1957-58), VA-176 (1958-60), VA-215 (1964-65), VA-145 (1965) and VA-152 (1966-67). The aircraft was transferred to the USAF in February 1968 and passed on to the VNAF.

## 7

**A-1J BuNo 142035/NL 204 of VA-165, USS Coral Sea (CVA-43), July 1965**

VA-165 replaced VA-152 in CVW-15 on board *Coral Sea* for the longest deployment – almost 11 months – of any air wing in the Vietnam War. This A-1 was delivered in October 1956, and it subsequently served with VA-216 (1956-58), VA-115 (1958-61), VA-215 (1961-63), VA-122 (1963-64), VA-165 (1964-65) and VA-215 (1966-67). Handed over to the USAF in November 1967, it was shot down over Laos on 8 December 1968 (as was the A-1 in Profile 24).

## 8

**EA-1F BuNo 132591/VR 707 of VAW-13 Det 1, 1965**

Most VAW-13 EA-1Fs operating on *Yankee Station* were sub-detachments of VAW-13 Det 1, permanently based at NAS Cubi Point. This EA-1F is unusual for a US Navy Skyraider in having a black-painted panel for disguising engine exhaust stains. Delivered to the US Navy as an AD-5N in October 1954, the aircraft served with VC-35 (1954-56), VMCJ-3 (1956-58, VA(AW)-35 (1958-59), VAW-33 (1959-61), VAW-11 (1961) and VAW-13 (1961-66). It is depicted here whilst embarked in USS *Independence* (CVA-62) with CVW-7 in the latter half of 1965. Transferred to VAW-33 in August 1966, the aircraft returned to the Tonkin Gulf with Det 11 as part of CVW-10 embarked in *Intrepid* in May 1967. BuNo 132591 was finally retired in July 1968.

## 9

**A-1H BuNo 139768/NE 577 of VA-25, USS Midway (CVA-41), September 1965**

This aircraft was flown by Lt Clint Johnson on 20 June 1965 over North Vietnam when he and Lt Charlie Hartman downed a VPAF MiG-17 during VA-25's first Vietnam deployment. Delivered to the US Navy in May 1956, it served with VA-42 (1956-59) and VA-122 (1960-64), prior to joining VA-25 in July 1964. Boasting a MiG-17 and two boat silhouettes beneath its cockpit, the combat veteran is also adorned with an impressive bomb tally. Passed on to VA-115 in September 1966, BuNo 139768 was downed off North Vietnam on 17 March 1967.

## 10

**A-1J BuNo 142051/AH 582 of VA-152, USS Oriskany (CVA-34), August 1965**

VA-152 replaced VA-165 in CVW-16 in 1964, and made all three of its Vietnam Skyraider deployments on *Oriskany*. This aircraft is armed with M116A2 napalm canisters as well as conventional 250-lb bombs. BuNo 142051 was delivered to the US Navy in December 1956 and subsequently served with VA-125 (1957), VA-155 (1957-58), VA-52 (1959), VA-95 (1959-61), VA-196 (1962-63), VA-95 once again (1963-64), VA-152 (1964-65) and VA-115 (1966). The A-1 was lost when it suffered engine

failure soon after launching from CVA-63 on *Yankee Station* on 19 May 1966.

## 11

**A-1H BuNo 139702/NM 601 of VA-196, USS Bon Homme Richard (CVA-31), October 1965**

After a quick turnaround, VA-196 returned to Vietnam zone in May 1965 for its last A-1 deployment. At 1000 lbs, the red-painted Mk 79 was the largest napalm bomb used by the US Navy in the Vietnam War. BuNo 139702 was delivered to the US Navy in February 1956, and duly served with VA-145 (1956-57), Marine Aircraft Repair Squadron (MARS) 17 (1957-58), VMA-322 (1958), VMA-331 (1958), VA-42 (1961), VA-85 (1961-62), VA-152 (1962-64), VA-163 (1964), VA-196 (1965-66), VA-145 (1966-67) and VA-176 (1967). BuNo 139702 was stricken two months later and acquired by the USAF. It was shot down over South Vietnam on 28 July 1971.

## 12

**A-1H BuNo 139692/NF 381 of VA-52, USS Ticonderoga (CVA-14), March 1966**

*THE WHIP* was assigned to Cdr John C Mape, who was killed in this A-1 by an SA-2 SAM over North Vietnam on 13 April 1966. Delivered to the US Navy in January 1956. BuNo 139692 served with VA-104 (1956-57), VA-15 (1958-59), VA-44 (1960), VA-35 (1960-61), VA-165 (1964-65) and VA-52 (1965-66).

## 13

**A-1H BuNo 139779/NE 574 of VA-25, USS Coral Sea (CVA-43), November 1966**

This aircraft was assigned to Lt Cdr Jim Ehret during VA-25's second Vietnam deployment, and its first on board *Coral Sea* with CVW-15. BuNo 139779 is also depicted in Profile 5.

## 14

**A-1J BuNo 142076/NH 502 of VA-115, USS Kitty Hawk (CVA-63), March 1966**

The Vietnam cruise of VA-115 on board CVA-63 was unique in that it was the only time that an A-1 unit deployed in a carrier air wing that also included an A-6 squadron (VA-85). BuNo 142076 was delivered to the US Navy in February 1957, and it served with VA-96 (1957-58), VA-126 (1958), VA-115 (1960-61), VA-25 (1961-62), VA-52 (1962-63), VA-115 (1964-67) and VA-25 (1967-68). Stricken in May 1968, BuNo 142076 was transferred to the USAF and written off in a crash-landing in South Vietnam in March 1972.

## 15

**A-1J BuNo 142016/NH501 of VA-115, USS Kitty Hawk (CVA-63), December 1965**

During its *Kitty Hawk* deployment, at least three VA-115 aircraft were painted with an experimental water-soluble green camouflage (FS34079 and FS34102). The underside remained white. The national insignia, large BuNo, modex and the word *NAVY* were all made smaller, and were applied with a more permanent paint. Tails codes were worn. Handed over to the US Navy in September 1956, this aircraft served with VX-5 (1956-58), VA-95

(1958-59), VA-122 (1959-62), VA-115 (1964-66), VA-122 (1966-67) and VA-145 (1967). BuNo 142016 was stricken and transferred to the USAF in January 1968, who later supplied it to the VNAF.

## 16

**A-1J BuNo 142031/NK 504 of VA-145, USS *Ranger* (CVA-61), February 1966**

This Skyraider was flown by Lt(jg) Dieter Dengler on his first, and only, mission over Indochina. He was shot down on 1 February 1966 during his ingress to the target, crash-landing in Laos. Delivered in October 1956, this A-1 served with VA-95 (1956-58), VA-25 (1960-62), VA-122 (1962), VA-196 (1963-64), VA-52 (1965) and VA-145 (1965-66).

## 17

**A-1H BuNo 137512/AH 504 of VA-152, USS *Oriskany* (CVA-34), August 1966**

This aircraft, serving with VA-152 during its second Vietnam deployment, features flash suppressors on the barrel tips of its 20 mm cannon to enhance pilot visual awareness during night operations. Delivered in January 1955, it served with VA-125 (1955-56), MARS-17 (1956), VMA-251 (1956), VA-215 (1957-59), VA-52 (1959), VA-35 (1961-62), VA-44 (1962-63), VA-15 (1963), VA-145 (1964-65) and VA-152 (1966-68). Transferred to the USAF in February 1968, the A-1 was lost over Laos on 4 July 1969.

## 18

**A-1J BuNo 142059/AK 204 of VA-165, USS *Intrepid* (CVS-11), October 1966**

*PUFF THE MAGIC DRAGON* was assigned to Lt Cdr 'Speed' Ritzman during VA-165's last A-1 Vietnam deployment. Delivered in December 1956, this aircraft served with VA-125 (1956-57), VA-155 (1957-58), VA-65 (1959), VA-25 (1959-60), VA-95 (1960-62), VA-165 (1963-66) and VA-215 (1967). Transferred to the USAF in August 1967, BuNo 142059 was shot down over South Vietnam on 7 May 1968.

## 19

**A-1H BuNo 137543/AK 409 of VA-176, USS *Intrepid* (CVS-11), October 1966**

This aircraft was used by Lt(jg) Tom Patton to down a MiG-17 on 6 October 1966. Teamed with VA-165 for the only dual-unit deployment for the A-1, VA-176 sported the most famous Skyraider marking of the war – the diving bee. VA-176 was the only A-1 unit to wear an 'X' marking on the base of the vertical stabiliser. It was used to calibrate the trim on the entire horizontal stabiliser, which was adjustable. It was also worn on the squadron's 1967 deployment to the Mediterranean. BuNo 137543 was delivered in March 1955 and served with VA-25 (1955-56), VA-175 (1957-58), VA-42 (1958), VA-85 (1959), VA-215 (1960-61), VA-122 (1961-64) and VA-176 (1965-66). Passed on to the USAF in February 1967, BuNo 137543 was shot down over Laos on 2 July 1969.

## 20

**A-1H BuNo 137586/NP 569 of VA-215, USS *Hancock* (CVA-19), April 1966**

This aircraft is carrying a typical RESCAP mission load-out – a centreline 300-gallon Aero 1 external fuel tank and two pods of 19 2.75-in folding-fin rockets. Built in May 1955, it served with VA-42 (1956), VA-75 (1956-57), VA-105 (1957-58), VA-165 (1958), VA-215 (1960-61), VT-30 (1962-64), VA-122 (1964-65), VA-215 (1965-66) and VA-176 (1967-68). BuNo 137586 was retired in early 1968.

## 21

**A-1H BuNo 137612/NF 504 of VA-115, USS *Hancock* (CVA-19), June 1967**

This aircraft, assigned to Lt Cdr Jack Jones, was adorned with three-toed black footprints painted on the fuselage and wings. It replaced BuNo 139768 in VA-115 as NF 504 after the ex-VA-25 MiG-killing A-1H was shot down on 17 March 1967. Delivered in July 1955, this aircraft served with VA-104 (1955-56), VA-175 (1956), VA-35 (1956-57), VA-85 (1957-58), VA-105 (1958-59), VA-94 (1959), VA-44 (1959-60), VA-176 (1960), VA-44 again (1960-61), VA-196 (1962-64), VA-25 (1966), VA-215 (1966) and VA-115 (1967). Handed over to the USAF in August 1967, BuNo 137612 was shot down over South Vietnam on 5 May 1968.

## 22

**A-1H BuNo 134569/NM 300 of VA-52, USS *Ticonderoga* (CVA-14), March 1967**

VA-52 was one of only three A-1 units in the Vietnam War to sport a 'CAG bird' (VA-165 and VA-196 were the others). It featured additional coloured stripes within its diagonal blue fuselage band to represent all of the squadrons in CVW-19. Its CAG assignment was also denoted by the lettering *COMATKCARAIRWING NINETEEN*. During this third, and last, Vietnam A-1 deployment for VA-52, all of its aircraft featured midnight blue weapon pylons inspired by the unit's Korean War lineage. Built in December 1953, this aircraft served with VF-194 (1954), VA-155 (1954-55), VA-125 (1956-57), VA-52 (1964-65), VA-122 (1965-66), VA-52 again (1966-67) and VA-152 (1967-68). Transferred to the USAF in February 1968, BuNo 134569 was passed on the VNAF and shot down in October 1972.

## 23

**A-1H BuNo 135324/NP 563 of VA-215, USS *Bonne Homme Richard* (CVA-31), May 1967**

VA-215 switched to CVA-31 for its third Vietnam deployment. Note the triangle marking above the tail code in red, with a black ball inside. BuNo 135324 was accepted by the US Navy in August 1954, and it served with VA-175 (1954-56), VMA-212 (1956-57), VA-195 (1958), VA-85 (1962-63), VA-42 (1963), VA-45 (1963-64), VA-25 (1964-66), VA-122 (1966) and VA-215 (1966-67). Passed on to the USAF in August 1967, the A-1 was shot down over South Vietnam on 18 June 1971.

## 24

**A-1J BuNo 142033/AK 501 of VA-145, USS *Intrepid* (CVS-11), September 1967**

*"Baby"* was assigned to the CO of VA-145, Cdr D E

Sparks, during the unit's last A-1 deployment. Delivered in October 1956, this aircraft served with VA-216 (1956-58), VA-126 (1958), VA-115 (1958-63), VA-152 (1963-64), VA-122 (1964-65), VA-165 (1965), VA-152 again (1965), VA-215 (1965-66), VA-122 (1966-67) and VA-145 (1967-68). Transferred to the USAF in February 1968, BuNo 142033 was shot down over Laos on 8 December 1969.

## 25

### A-1H BuNo 134575/AH 511 of VA-152, USS Oriskany (CVA-34), November 1967

*FOO FOO JUICE* features a yellow tail cap applied for VA-152's last Vietnam Skyraider deployment, for which the unit's A-1s were fitted with Yankee rocket extraction seats. BuNo 134575 was built in December 1953 and served with VA-115 (1954-55), VA-196 (1956-57), VA-42 (1959-61), VA-65 (1963), VA-145 (1965), VA-52 (1965-66) and VA-152 (1966-68). Acquired by the USAF in March 1968, it was transferred to the VNAF and lost on 21 June 1974.

## 26

### EA-1F BuNo 132591/AK 783 of VAW-33 Det 11, USS Intrepid (CVS-11), November 1967

Det 11 deployed with three EA-1Fs in CVW-10 during CVS-11's second Vietnam cruise. EA-1Fs in the combat zone were armed with one 20 mm cannon in each wing. Note the *Tonkin Gulf Yacht Club* patch above the national insignia. Delivered in October 1954, this aircraft served with VC-35 (1954-56), VMCJ-3 (1956-58), VA(AW)-35 (1958-59), VAW-33 (1959-61), VAW-11 (1961), VAW-13 (1961-66) and VAW-33 (1966-68). It was retired in July 1968.

## 27

### A-1H BuNo 135300/NL 405 of VA-25, USS Coral Sea (CVA-43), January 1968

During VA-25's third, and last, Vietnam deployment in A-1s, this aircraft – assigned to Lt(jg) Dale Pellott – flew the final combat sortie by the attack version of the US Navy Skyraider. Delivered in June 1954, it flew with VA-55 (1954-56), VA-115 (1956-58), VA-145 (1962-63), VA-25 (1964-66), VA-52 (1966-67) and VA-25 again (1967-68). The A-1 was retired to the Naval Aviation Museum at Pensacola in April 1968.

## 28

### EA-1F BuNo 132555/VR 012 of VAW-13, USS Kitty Hawk (CVA-63), May 1968

This VAW-13 detachment was unusual in that it deployed with CVA-63 directly from NAS Alameda, rather than being a sub-det of Det 1 at Cubi Point. Delivered in February 1954, this aircraft served with VC-33 (1954-56), VMCJ-3 (1956-58), VAW-33 (1959-64), VAW-33 (1964-66) and VAW-13 (1966-68). BuNo 132555 was retired in August 1968.

## 29

### EA-1F BuNo 134974/NM 705 of VAQ-33 Det 14, USS Ticonderoga (CVA-14), June 1968

Det 14 was the only VAW/VAQ-33 unit to deploy on a Pacific Fleet carrier during the Vietnam War. By the time of this cruise, VAW-33 had been redesig-nated VAQ-33, and EA-1Fs from VAW-13 were being phased out in favour of EKA-3Bs. This aircraft was delivered in January 1955, and served with VC-35 (1955-56), VMC-1 (1956-57), VA(AW)-33 (1958), VA(AW)-35 (1958-59), VAW-33 (1959), VAW-13 (1960-67) and finally VAQ-33 (1967-69). It was stricken in June 1969.

## 30

### EA-1F BuNo 132545/AK 601 of VAQ-33 Det 11, USS Intrepid (CVS-11), December 1968

Det 11 deployed with CVW-10 on board *Intrepid* for the carrier's third, and final, Vietnam cruise, and made the final US Navy combat deployment of the Skyraider. At some point during the deployment, the modex series for the det changed from 600 to 800. Built in July 1954, this aircraft served with VMC/VMCJ-3 (1954-56), VA(AW)-35 (1957-58), Pacific Missile Range (1958-62), VAW-33 (1962-65), VAW-13 (1965-67) and VAQ-33 (1967-69). It too was retired in June 1969.

# COLOUR SECTION

## 1

A VAW-11 Det Q EA-1E radar early warning aircraft assigned to USS *Bennington* (CVS-20) in May 1965. The four-seat EA-1E was approaching retirement as the Vietnam War heated up, and served over the Tonkin Gulf only into 1965. It was replaced by the E-1B Tracer on ASW carriers (*Richard W Albright via Wayne Mutza collection*)

## 2

A VA-196 A-1J assigned to the 'Main Battery's' CO, Cdr J R Driscoll, displays a full wing load of ordnance on CVA-31 in preparation for a mission over Laos in late 1964. The folding wing section hosts three 260-lb fragmentation bombs and three 5-in HVARs. The latter were being phased out in favour of the folding-fin Zuni rockets. The folding wing section lacks the 20 mm cannon normally installed. (*Paul Rhodes via Wayne Mutza collection*)

## 3

A VA-196 A-1H parked on the deck of CVA-31 during a port call in Yokosuka, Japan, in late 1964, after leaving the Tonkin Gulf and *Yankee Team* mission over Laos. VA-196 was the only Vietnam-era A-1 VA squadron to use the 600-series for its modex. The Aero 1 external tanks are painted gull grey on top instead of white – unusual for the Skyraider (*Paul Rhodes via Wayne Mutza collection*)

## 4

A VAW-13 EA-1F see in 1966 parked on the apron a Da Nang AB – a common alternate airfield for carrier-based aircraft in the Tonkin Gulf. During the mid-1960s, Det 1 aircraft wore modex numbers in the 770-780 series, and kept the VR tail code regardless of which air wing they were seconded to (*Tom Hansen via Wayne Mutza collection*)

**5**
The open rear compartment hatches on this VAW-13 Det 1 EA-1F at Da Nang in 1966 show the seats of the enlisted electronic warfare operators, as well as the electronic equipment mounted behind them. Visible on the ventral fuselage are the two direction-finding antenna domes. The 'pigtail' cable connecting the ALT-2/7 jamming pod with the aircraft's wiring can be seen under the wing (*Tom Hansen via Wayne Mutza collection*)

**6**
The port wing of this VA-152 'Spad' on board CVA-34 is loaded with a Mk 77 Mod 0 750-lb napalm canister and four 500-lb high-drag bombs (*Gary Gottschalk via Wayne Mutza collection*)

**7**
VA-196 ordnancemen James Hannan and Paul Rhodes pose with the fruits of their labour – a full load for this 'Main Battery' A-1H, which was assigned to Cdr Joseph Gallagher during the squadron's 1965 deployment to Vietnam. The 'Spad' is loaded with red-painted Mk 79 1000-lb napalm canisters on the inboard wing stations and 12 250-lb bombs on the outboard wing pylons. The payload capacity of the A-1 kept ordnancemen both busy and fit (*Paul Rhodes via W Mutza collection*)

**8**
A section of VA-152 Skyraiders return from a mission during the squadron's first Southeast Asia deployment in 1965. The A-1J (foreground) flies wing on the A-1H. Note the unusual grey rudder on the A-1H. Most control surfaces on US Navy Skyraiders of the period were painted white (*Gary Gottschalk via Wayne Mutza collection*)

**9**
An A-1J of VA-145 prepares to launch from the No 4 catapult of CVA-61 (*US Navy via John Eckberg*)

**10**
This A-1J (BuNo 142028) replaced A-1H BuNo 134472 in VA-176 as AK 402 (assigned to Cdr Ray Ashworth) after the latter made a gear-up landing on *Intrepid* on 19 July 1966. The aircraft's cannons are tipped with flash suppressors for night operations (*Tom Hansen via Wayne Mutza collection*)

**11**
A-1J BuNo 142059 *PUFF THE MAGIC DRAGON* was assigned to Lt Cdr 'Speed' Ritzmann of VA-165. It is seen here after recovering at Da Nang AB on 10 September 1966 following a 4.6-hour RESCAP mission. Note the impressive array of mission markings under the cockpit. Ritzmann would subsequently fly with VA-25 during the US Navy's last attack Skyraider combat deployment (*Tom Hansen via Wayne Mutza collection*)

**12**
This VA-152 A-1H was seen from the USAF HU-16B that it was escorting on a RESCAP mission over the Tonkin Gulf in September 1966. This aircraft, assigned to *Jimbo*, is marked with three Purple Heart medals on the lower section of the engine cowling (*Tom Hansen via Wayne Mutza collection*)

**13**
Two VA-152 'Spads' on a stopover at Da Nang AB. Except for the usual exhaust stains on the forward fuselage, the aircraft in the foreground is exceptionally clean. During the squadron's 1966 Vietnam Skyraider deployment, the 'Wild Aces' switched from a large yellow chevron tail marking to the smaller one seen here above the tail code (*Tom Hansen via Wayne Mutza collection*)

**14**
A VA-25 A-1H escorts an HU-16B over the Tonkin Gulf during the unit's second Vietnam deployment in 1966 (*Tom Hansen via Wayne Mutza collection*)

**15**
Another VA-25 A-1H – this one assigned to Lt Cdr Jim Ehret – flies wing on an HU-16B over the Tonkin Gulf in 1966. The squadron's Battle Excellence 'E' award is painted behind the cockpit (*Tom Hansen via Wayne Mutza collection*)

**16**
A VA-25 A-1H flies wing on a HU-16B over a cloudy Tonkin Gulf in December 1966. Pairs of US Navy 'Spads' were routinely assigned RESCAP missions to protect the Albatrosses during their rescue attempts for downed aircrews in the gulf (*Tom Hansen via Wayne Mutza collection*)

**17**
This VA-52 A-1H (BuNo 135332), shown in late 1966 or early 1967, is armed with eight seven-shot pods of 2.75-in folding-fin aerial rockets. It survived service with the US Navy, USAF and VNAF, and was purchased from Thailand after the war. It flies as a warbird under private ownership in the US (*Tom Hansen via Wayne Mutza collection*)

**18**
The 'Fists of the Fleet' wardroom poses with one of its 'Spads' on the deck of CVA-43 during VA-25's third Vietnam deployment in 1967-68. The CO, Cdr Cliff Church, if fifth from left, kneeling. One of the co-authors, Lt Cdr 'Zip' Rausa, is eighth from left, standing. Lt(jg) Ted Hill, who flew the attack A-1's last US Navy sortie, is standing, far right (*US Navy via Rosario Rausa*)

**19**
VA-176 A-1H assigned to MiG-killer Lt Peter F Russell on the deck of *Saratoga* in 1967 during the last attack Skyraider deployment to the Mediterranean. Russell later joined VAL-4 in South Vietnam and was killed while flying an OV-10A Bronco on 23 May 1969 (*Angelo Gialanella via Angelo Romano*)

# INDEX

References to illustration captions are shown in **bold**. Plates are prefixed pl and followed by the page number in brackets upon which its caption appears.